The Liberation of Work

The Liberation of Work

*The Elimination of Strikes and Strife in Industry
through associative Organization of Enterprise*

FOLKERT WILKEN

ROY PUBLISHERS, INC.
NEW YORK 10021

Translated from the German Die Befreiung der Arbeit
© *Verlag Die Kommenden 1965*

© *Routledge & Kegan Paul Ltd. 1969*

Library of Congress Catalog Card No 70-98423

Printed in Great Britain

Preface

by

E. F. SCHUMACHER

All wealth stems from human work applied to the facilities offered by Nature. If the work is well done, intelligently done, generously and freely made available to fit the objective requirements of a given situation, then the creation of material well-being is no serious problem. On the other hand, if work is reluctantly or sullenly offered, irresponsibly performed, skimped and starved, all economic problems become difficult, if not insoluble.

Fortunately, man does not merely like to work, his happiness is absolutely dependent on it. He needs an outlet for his energies; he needs to utilize and develop his potential; he needs to join with other men for mutual stimulation in productive companionship. These are overpowering needs, and a man faces virtual destruction if they cannot be met. He may find this or that substitute, this or that palliative; but not for long. To be without work—which is not the same as being without employment—is slow death, just like being without food, only slower.

The human stage, therefore, is set for the creation of wealth, inasmuch as wealth presupposes man's work, and work is what man needs for his happiness even more than he needs wealth.

And yet, work in modern society all too often has a bad name. It does not flow freely, and, as a result, there is frustration, unhappiness, and economic trouble. The obvious truth that people like to work is an unpopular truth, generally treated with derision, if not with hostility. To introduce labour-saving devices; to reduce the hours of work, to promote job elimination and automation—all this is 'progress'. It is the ideal of the employer to have output without workers, and of the worker to have income without work. The real task, we are told, is to educate people 'for leisure'. But what does that mean? It means to educate them in such a way that they will know what to do with their leisure time,

v

because idleness would obviously destroy them. In other words : education for leisure means education for self-chosen work, or it means nothing at all.

However that may be, for the present, at any rate, there is plenty of work to be done. Even in the so-called affluent societies the problems of production have by no means been solved; there is still poverty, gross neglect, even hunger. On a world scale, there are today more destitute people than ever before in history, only partly due to swollen populations. Before we talk too loudly about education for leisure, we ought to face the problem of work : how to 'liberate' work, so that it will flow freely, happily, creatively, with a minimum of hindrance and frustration.

Professor Wilken's book on 'The Liberation of Work' is therefore greatly to be welcomed.

If the problem of work is treated as primarily a problem of economics it becomes insoluble; for it is a much deeper matter than anything economics is able to deal with. What is it then? Professor Wilken knows that it is an intensely philosophical, not to say a 'religious' problem. He is not afraid to discuss his subject in terms of ultimate human values, because 'in *human* activity, behind all muscular and cerebral functioning, there works the spiritual impulse of the human ego, which alone gives labour dignity. Labour should never, therefore, be treated as merchandise. If it is, human dignity is always violated, and the result of this is that devotion to work is undermined. Only prostitution to materialist interests can render the human worker more or less insensitive to this injury to his personality, but such interests cannot wipe out the results : antipathy and apathy'.

Professor Wilken's book, however, would fail to rise above the general level of *Kulturkritik*, certainly legitimate but all too frequently sterile, if it shied away from tough problems of social organization; for there can be no liberation of work without justice, and 'responsible economic justice can only be achieved by social methods'. Happily, he does not shy away.

The unit most in need of new social methods is undoubtedly the individual enterprise, the firm. It is here that the search for a new concept of labour relations has to take place with a view to achieving, what Professor Wilken calls, 'solidarity between entrepreneurs and workers'.

At the level of national politics, there may be a solidarity of the entrepreneurs and a solidarity of the workers, but these two separate solidarities can only play havoc at the level of the firm, where a quite different 'solidarity of partnership' is needed. What, then, could bring about the solidarity, or partnership, between entrepreneurs and workers? This is the whole crux of the matter and must be the starting point of all constructive social-political thought.

The broad generalizations of the political debate—capitalism vs. socialism, planning vs. the free market; etc. etc.—are today worse than useless. We have to come to grips with the precise details of the social situation, with the precise rights and obligations of the persons or groups involved; with real 'constitution-making' for various types of firms and other associations below the level of the state. What becomes of the idea of ownership, once ownership ceases to be wholly personal? Personal (or private) ownership is a *bundle* of rights and obligations, and when there is any change away from the personal (or private) level, every one of the specific rights and obligations making up the 'bundle' must be separately studied and separately 'placed' with persons, groups, or other organizations capable of exercising such rights and obligations and interested in doing so. This requires painstaking work of a highly inventive and imaginative kind, based not only on solid practical knowledge but also on a firm conviction of the ultimate value of the human person.

Ingenuity is needed, but so is compassion. Practical realism is needed, but so is philosophy. A merely positivistic approach is useless because the present system fails to 'liberate work' and too often prevents people from realizing their potential; but a merely idealistic approach is equally useless because, while social arrangements can give people room for stretching and widening their personalities, they cannot overcome the inherent weakness of human nature which produces an incalculable gap between potential and actual.

We can be grateful, therefore, that Professor Wilken has taken the trouble not only of exposing the problems but also of collecting a number of case studies to show how actual firms in this actual world have tried—and are trying—to develop new modes of co-operation and associative partnership in business. Let us hope that there will be much more experimentation in this field in the future. It is hard work, but what could be the fate of industrial society if this work failed to be done? Would it get stuck in 'antipathy and apathy'? Or would it end in a kind of suicidal revolt of affronted human dignity against inhuman forms of social organization—forms which appear to serve 'efficiency' but in fact lose even efficiency when they fail to serve humanity? The industrialized world is not lacking in signs that such a revolt could happen before long.

Finally, then, would it not be advisable for industrial societies, which so implicitly believe in research of all kinds, to set aside substantial funds for *action research* in this all important field? Where Zeiss, Bosch, Lewis, Bader and others have privately blazed a new trail, is it not time that this work became the concern of all of us, backed by our collective institutions?

5 June 1968

Contents

Introduction   xi

I The Labour-Market, an Economic Contradiction
and a Social Fallacy

The labour-market and labour morals   1
The labour-market, in the light of full employment   5
*The effects of the labour-market on the structure of
the enterprise*   8
A just income structure   12
The workers' claims to the profits   15
Rival claims on capital   17

II Capital Ownership and the Sources of Income

The entrepreneur as trustee   21
The neutralization of capital   24
*The relation of capital neutralization to a just income
structure*   26

III The Search for a New Social Concept of Labour
Relations

Solidarity between entrepreneur and workers   30
Ownership of the means of production   32
*The physical and human polarities within an enter-
prise*   33
The operation of the working community   35

IV The Workers' Responsibilities

The separation of work and income   39
Putting this separation into practice   41

V Trade Unions and a New Social Order

The social unification of the workers 44
Industrial democracy and nationalization, as trade union goals 46
The true responsibilities of the trade unions 51
Co-operation between trade unions and working-communities 54

VI Stages in the Constitution of the Enterprise

The commercial conception of the enterprise 59
The business partnership: Gert Spindler and shared-enterprise 60
The G. L. Rexroth Ironworks 67
The associative business: integration of Scott Bader and Co. 68
Associative enterprise and associative economy 73
The 'democratic' principle in industry 74
The John Lewis Partnership, London 81

VII Socialization in Germany

The Volkswagen Foundation 90
The Staedtler Foundation 91
The Carl Zeiss Foundation 95
The Robert Bosch Trust 96
Summary of methods of neutralizing capital and administering profits 98

Conclusion 102

References 105

Note on the author 106

Index 107

Some chapters at the end of the book have been omitted as they deal mainly with specific German situations.

Introduction

The economic system is a continual struggle to maintain two separate states of balance. One is the balance between consumption and production. The other is the balance between prices and income, and thus between the rate of production and the rate of income capable of absorbing the total supply.

The problem we shall deal with here stems from the fundamental law, that consumption and production must be made to balance. Materially, this balance is one between the quantity of consumption and the quantity of production. But the material quantitative factors demanding this balance are merely the outward expression of qualitative social factors, which are at the root of the quantitative. The needs of the individual are of great human importance, but the needs of a community of individuals, all depending on one another, take on a *social* significance. This leads to the question: is it befitting to human dignity, that one section of humanity should live in luxury, another section have at any rate enough to live on, while a greater proportion must support themselves on less than a living wage, and a further section is left to starve? This is the vital social question underlying the economic satisfaction of needs. Of a different nature is the social problem connected with the *production* of the goods demanded. Here comes into account the fact that human beings must co-operate in a decent fashion, to produce the goods demanded by the system.

Modern economists have, on the whole, been unable to discover social formulas by which co-operation in the economic field may become truly communal. For such co-operation calls for an economic system based on division of labour and unity of all spheres of labour. Not the principle of co-operation, however, but that of competition, governs the system created by Western civilization. The market policy aims at mastering every economic situation, and subjecting all economic activity to this principle of competition. This principle is essentially *anti-social*, and aims at achieving an integrated economy by competition in the various markets. The organization of human labour has also been subjected to it, and this affects the production of goods to meet human needs. The policy of competition is the policy of a selfish law of supply. It does not achieve a real supply of essentials, a supply which would embrace the needs of all mankind.

The competitive method of labour organization tends to affect indirectly the balance between prices and income, continually disturbing this balance, or even preventing its being established at all. The alarming thing about the present wage disputes is the fact that higher wages and shorter hours, and thus lowered production, have brought rising prices in their wake. As far as possible, industry has passed on to her customers the expenses laid on her by the Trade Unions. Moreover, pay-rises carried through in one place are automatically followed by similar increases in other parts of the system. For example, in the mining industry, wages were increased regardless of the unfavourable state of profits. To fulfil the Union's wage demands, the industry demanded higher subsidies from the government, and thus from tax-payers in general. Another instance is the paper industry. It, too, was motivated in its price increases by increases in pay. These increased paper prices, in their turn, raise the price of books, periodicals, and newspapers, which must themselves then reckon with rising wages. So, too, have the railways and the postal service increased their rates, chiefly on grounds of increased wages.

The disturbances in the economic balance resulting from excessive rates of pay and cutting of hours are not taken very seriously by the workers. They wish to prove that their policy of wage claims is justified, and point out the general inflationary tendencies to which, throughout the world, the economic structure is subject. But these wage disputes, which in their unreasonableness yet contain some element of justice, can never lead to social harmony because the underlying problems determining them are not touched on at all.

The trouble behind the increasing demands continually being pressed by the workers, looked into more deeply, lies in a sense of injustice. This springs from the position they occupy in the system. But such demands for justice spring from the deepest recesses of the human soul, where is rooted the indestructible germ of *humanity*. The realization of social justice is valued higher than any economic disturbances arising from its attainment. Of a very different nature is the motive behind the opposition of the entrepreneurs and employers to increased pay and shorter hours. *Their* attitude is inspired by the interest they have in upholding the market-dominated system, and the rights of ownership which are rooted in this. They would like to justify this system which is to blame for the wage disputes, and to save it from the consequences of its basic principle, which arose when the principle of selfish satisfaction of the needs of the individual consumer was transformed into the guiding principle of the whole economic process. As this principle is in its very essence antisocial, the State has been allotted the task of correcting the economic and social harm caused by this anti-social principle, by taking on itself the function of the essential binding social element. Thus the State is charged with the social responsibility for the realization of social values in an economic system which can achieve the ideal of freedom only in an anti-social way, carrying competition even into those spheres which lie outside the exchange of commodities. To these spheres belongs the labour-market, on which the rival instincts for gain of both parties explode in industrial strife. This strife is waged with economic weapons, and only in extreme circumstances does the violence of the underlying factors reveal itself.

What are these underlying factors? What are the real driving compulsions? And what do economic reason and social truth demand? How can human labour be fitted into the economic process without strife? The following enquiries will endeavour to find social formulas by which labour may be assimilated into the economic body, organically, in other words, without conflict.

I

The Labour-Market, an Economic Contradiction and a Social Fallacy

THE LABOUR-MARKET AND LABOUR MORALS

Under the influence of the economic system, swayed only by the interests of capital and gain, human labour is organized in such a way that it, too, is controlled by desire for gain.

The method developed by this system, to make its own functioning possible, is the market. Hence it is called market-economy, to distinguish it from economic planning by the government. The market is, indeed, a social phenomenon, but one in which the social factor which binds human beings together is reduced to a bare minimum, in other words, to a technical contract in which humanity is not taken into account, apart from the observance of the contract's clauses. The market on which this substitute for the human bond does at least go through the accepted motions of fulfilling these obligations, is the product-market. Here, money is exchanged for material goods, that is, products. In the product-market, the person offering the goods has no interest in them at all, except in their countervalue. The purchaser, of course, has a considerable interest in the goods, but he also has an equal interest in the money he must hand over for them. Thus, on the product-market, selfish mercenary interest rules both parties. A personal interest in the intrinsic value of the goods inspires the buyer only, not the seller.

This fact is significant, if we wish to form a true estimate of the *labour-market*. On the product-market, goods of a material kind are traded, that is, goods to which there pertains nothing of *humanity*. But on the labour-market, *human* material, that is, strength and skill, is bargained for as a commodity. This means that here both buyer and seller of this living merchandise are motivated by those very considerations which are justifiable only

1

in the product-market. But on the labour-market, they destroy humanity, degrading it. The seller of strength and skill is under the sway of the product-market, and can therefore have no *human* interest in his ability and skill. He is interested solely in their countervalue, in the form of wages. Moreover, he behaves in this respect like the merchant in the product-market, in the intention of giving away as little work as possible in return for his price. Thus, the workers, supported by the Unions, have always two aims: to give as little work as possible, for as high a wage as possible. This is done by continually cutting down working hours, while maintaining the high wage, or raising it still further. Such an aspiration conforms to the philosophy of the product-market, developed by the principle of egotism, and seen from the supplier's standpoint. The government, permitting this market system, sanctions this state of affairs, and has virtually raised it to the status of an accepted law, which is scientifically termed the principle of market 'mechanism'.

When human labour is organized by such a method as this, the inevitable result is that the worker adopts such an attitude to his work that he does it, not for its own sake, but for the sake of payment. According to market philosophy, the urge to work arises solely from the need for money, and the material desires connected with money. This philosophy inevitably undermines the free willingness to work, and leads to a misunderstanding of the responsibility which Man's destiny has laid upon him. The market is therefore a personal and a social disaster. The social critique levelled by Karl Marx at the capitalist system culminates in the accusation that it treats human labour as a commodity. At first, the workers revolted against this, from an injured sense of human dignity. Today, however, it has come to this—that the workers, and their mouthpiece the Trade Unions, acknowledge the fact that labour is being commercialized, and accept it as a *fait accompli*. The worker has been brought by the labour-market to the point where he is indifferent both to his work, and to its barter as merchandise, and, inspired solely by greed, he would like to lead the contented and continually expanding life of a consumer. Best of all, he would like to acquire wealth without working—a desire in which he is vindicated by those publicly sanctioned institutions, Premium Bonds, the Pools, Bingo, etc. This anti-social method of labour organization has very far-reaching consequences, which have an obstructive effect on the development of the worker's character.

To estimate fully the disastrous effect this has on the attitude of the worker towards his work, deeper understanding is needed of the *meaning* work has for the worker. Each worker should feel that work is his elixir of life, and that through the application it demands, his personality is formed, strengthened, and developed. Because this is so, by nature Man works willingly. When he works, he activates and concentrates the spiritual part of his being, his innermost self. In work, the human ego expresses itself, and thus the essential nature of humanity itself is revealed. The nature of the work, so long as it is suited to the individual's abilities, is not important. Its strength does not lie only in muscle or in brain. These can, if necessary, be traded, just as we set animals to work for us. But in *human* activity, behind all muscular and cerebral functioning, there works the spiritual impulse of the human self, which alone gives labour dignity. Labour should never, therefore, be treated as merchandise. If it is, human dignity is always violated, and the result of this is that devotion to work is undermined. Only prostitution to materialistic interests can render the human worker more or less insensitive to this injury to his personality, but such interests cannot wipe out the results: antipathy and apathy.

Today it is no simple task to free labour from its subjugation to materialism. The system set up by capitalist ideology as the labour-market finds an ally in the materialistic outlook of the modern worker. This outlook directly stems from the natural will to survive of the human being, who must build up and secure a material existence for himself, by toil. This will to survive then naturally becomes an incentive to work, and is inextricably bound up with it, when the individual is self-employed. In this case, when he is working only for himself, the fruits of his labour become his own property. Here, self-interested work is still done willingly, without discord. However, the economic system is such that the achievements of labour are greater when they profit other people, and are not retained by the worker. The slogan, division of labour, contains a great social law, traceable in the very creation of the world itself. It was called by Rudolph Steiner, 'The fundamental law of Society'.

This law, according to Rudolph Steiner, runs thus: 'The

welfare of a human community, working together, is so much the greater, the less each individual lays claim to the proceeds of his own labour, and the more he gives away to his fellow-workers, and the more his own needs are satisfied by the output of the others, rather than by his own. Any institution conflicting with this law must, in the long run, in some way, breed misery and want.' When a man does not keep the fruits of his labour for himself, but gives them up to others, he makes a sacrifice. In such deeds lies a special source of power, not generally recognized, for the doer himself. But this is only so, when it is done in a corresponding *spirit*. Acts of generosity are the greatest means of increasing men's moral strength. This is always synonymous with the development of *character*, for example, rendering it capable of enduring hard times, and the blows of misfortune, which men who strive only after material power, whether it be money or muscle, mental skill or personal prestige, could never endure. Also, people inspired by the spirit of that fundamental law of society have a socially formative effect on their surroundings. They become creative in all fields, and extend the bounds of their awareness, to such a degree that they introduce the right developments into whatever sphere they find themselves occupying. Such people never compromise with the confirmed materialists, who can think only in material terms, and act only according to materialistic principles which they have formulated as dogmas.

Thus, according to the law of division of labour, human toil must be organized in such a way that its fruits benefit others. Moreover, in this law, there is the incentive to the worker that he can accelerate and strengthen his personal development to the greatest extent, if only he can accomplish his work *objectively*, by acts of selflessness.

The prospect of this is ruined by the state of the labour-market, and the corresponding attitude of the worker towards his work. He does this work subjectively, that is, mainly for himself, not for others. Therefore, he demands the highest possible wage, and tends to give as little work as possible. This is the tragedy of labour morals in the modern system. It lies in the destruction of the natural urge for self-expression, by which all work should be motivated. It is a blow at the foundations of the economic structure, which is based on the principle of freedom. What Marx labelled as exploitation merely meant that the commodity, labour, was too poorly paid. Today this is obviously no longer the case. But the labour-market still continues, and with it the moral servitude of the human spirit, through the market's control over the organization of labour. State-control of industry, in the Eastern bloc, subjugates the spirit just as strongly, to all appearances more strongly. On the other hand, it is noteworthy that in the East, the emphasis is laid on human achievement, and it is continually claimed that this is accomplished freely and gladly, indeed, that it is increasing more and more in the service of the community. In the Western market system, on the contrary, the Trade Unions never speak of achievement, but always of the payment for achievement, and of reducing performance. This is because they do not have the right attitude to their work. But that is the fault of the labour-market.

THE LABOUR-MARKET, IN THE LIGHT OF FULL EMPLOYMENT

It is sometimes said that the dependence of the worker on a capitalist has been largely surmounted, and that the labour-market has ceased to be what Marx once represented it. That the structure of the labour-market remains unchanged, is shown when so-called full employment is reached, and becomes over-employment. This gives the workers a monopoly. This situation has occurred in present times. It clearly reveals the deterioration of labour morals is brought about by the labour market.

Of course, full employment is a social ideal. But it assumes that every able-bodied man has gained a place in the social system. In this place, he serves by his labour society as a whole and receives from the labour of the others everything that he needs for his support. The social harmony of labour, each for all, attains in full employment the state of a socially well-ordered administration. However, in a system where the labour-market negotiates employment, full employment produces on this market a boom in the labour supply. There arise fluctuations in the economic ratio of values, when the demand for labour exceeds the supply. Then, exactly the same thing happens as on the product-markets in such circumstances. A commodity which is demanded beyond the available supply rises in exchange value. This is effected either by raising its price or by supplying fewer goods for the same price. On the product-markets, this is a reasonable and scientific procedure. But on the labour-market, it is absurd, socially speaking, for an increased demand for labour to result in an increase of pay. Economically considered, it leads to fluctuations in income, or to an increase in prices. Anyone who exploits his power in the labour-market, either as customer or as supplier, employer or employee, blackmails the other party, in the first instance by wage-skimping, in the second by exorbitant wage demands. He thus obtains a higher income at the expense of the other party. Apart from this, the general attitude of the labour-market has a particularly degrading effect on the work morals of a great many workers. An article in the *Deutsche Zeitung* (12/8/62) says, 'Lack of enthusiasm, declining discipline, and shoddy workmanship are here, as elsewhere, the consequences of uninterrupted full employment. In other countries also, employment and labour morals stand in the same perverted relationship. This can be tolerated, so long as it remains within definite bounds. But the extent to which our production is slowing down is gradually reaching dangerous proportions. For it is infecting the mass of people still doing good work.'

From these conditions, it comes about that the worker has no *awareness* of, and therefore no *interest* in, the factors surrounding his work. The market-controlled income structure destroys the wage-earner's awareness that his existence is rooted in a higher economic whole, in which he works, and to whose prosperity his work contributes. Between this higher whole and his job arbitrates the court of the labour-market, in which the demand side, in the form of private enterprise, is also controlled not by the higher whole, but by the interests of the entrepreneur. The special function of the entrepreneur consists, then, in his utilization of the market-regulated proceeds of labour, in the larger context of the product-market. Thus, in a purely selfish way, he adapts himself to the higher economic whole. But the awareness and interest of the worker, concentrating strictly on the task of the moment, does not extend to the utilization of his achievements on the market, in their wider economic significance. Moreover, he fulfils his tasks because he is *compelled* to do so, to keep his job. It is the narrowness of market mentality which is to blame for the worker's lack of interest in the economic system as a whole, and for the fact that he can therefore feel no interest in his work, except for its payment. From this indifference and ignorance of the personal and social value of work, grows the selfish instinct, conforming to that of the market, to do as little work as possible, but to preserve the wages already attained, and if possible to raise them still further. Shorter hours and longer paid holidays do not make good sense, economically speaking, unless performance is sufficiently productive to justify this. This much-discussed problem needs to be still more closely examined.

The worker's inability to develop a proper attitude to his work, owing to the philosophy of the labour-market, renders him indifferent as to whether the business for which he works prospers or runs into difficulties. As he has no inspiring awareness of the higher issues on which his existence depends, he feels no *sense of solidarity* with all those who work in the economic organization, or who control it so as to make possible the material existence of all who belong to the social organism. As a rule, he does not even feel any unity with the company which has bought his services. He demands that it shall give him as high a wage as possible, and grant as short hours as possible. But socially, it is vital that the worker should be so placed in the activities of his company that he cannot help experiencing some sort of impulse of shared responsibility not determined by mercenary interest. In the American Trade Unions, so keenly do they apply themselves to labour politics, there exists this idea of economic solidarity, which leads them to feel concern for the success of the company for which they have helped to procure labour. If necessary, they even subsidize struggling companies with an injection of capital.

The *economic and social unawareness* of these confirmed egotists is blatantly revealed when workers in a struggling company actually demand higher wages, and go on strike to obtain these. This economically paradoxical behaviour is made possible by the fact that it originates, not in the personal motives of the individual worker, but from the aims of that impersonal abstraction, the Trade Unions. The Unions, in exploiting the power they have on the market, act according to the rules of the game, as laid down by the labour-market.

THE EFFECTS OF THE LABOUR-MARKET ON THE
STRUCTURE OF THE ENTERPRISE

The trader-like attitude shown in the recruiting of workers does not originally come from the worker, but from the employer and entrepreneur, whose thoughts are ruled completely by the market, and who can think only in terms of merchandise. It is the entrepreneur who creates the atmosphere in which the work is carried out, by his commercial attitude. This atmosphere is lacking in all human warmth, all social relations. It is composed merely of the abstract relationship of performance and payment. It was this commercial spirit which created the labour-market, and it penetrates deep into the heart of industry, and here finally reveals its completely *anti-social* nature, which prevents the worker from freely developing his personality. It is this which makes it impossible for him to feel unity with the economy as a whole, or even with the enterprise for which he works, and to take his share of responsibility for its prosperity.

If it is insane, humanly and socially, to degrade labour to a marketable commodity, so it is also quite justifiable to treat the *product* of the labour as a commodity, being the achievement embodied in a material object, and to pay for it as such. In short, not the labour, but the achievement accomplished by it, is a commodity. A woman hemming handkerchiefs, at home, is paid for the results of her work, not for the time and effort she put into them. The effort partakes of something personal, and cannot be paid for in money, but the solid results can be bought from her.

Paying a worker exactly according to results is difficult in the case of a group of men working together, under a supervisor, on a technical job, thus availing themselves of the machinery and instruments. There are, indeed, activities which can here be attributed to the individual worker, for instance, work with the lathe, and can be paid for accordingly. This is done by the system of *piecework wages*. But there are activities, such as work at the conveyor-belt, or in book-keeping, which cannot be individually attributed and separately paid. Here the situation is usually overcome by payment per hour. But the fact must not be overlooked that, in both cases the worker is being drawn into the business, and thus placed in a greater context, which forces him to achievement. It is often said that the moment the worker enters the factory his freedom is at an end. This is an exageration, for it is only that his free willingness to work, to express himself, is now subordinated to supervision and the rules of the production processes.

This circumstance may be treated materially or organically, that is, socially. *Materially* considered, it leads to the situation we find ourselves in today. The material goal of productivity is accepted. Impetus is provided by the entrepreneur and the management. Execution is carried out by the workers, and by the machinery. The machinery is bought, and the achievement of the workers using it is also bought. The entire process of the productive function is thus analysed into its separate elements and seen in the light of accountability.

Organically considered another picture presents itself. The social mentality conceives the business enterprise as a single unit. The entire unit is constituted as a dynamic organism. At the head there is the all-embracing guiding spirit branching out into subordinate levels of management. The whole body aims at transforming raw materials into useful products. This process depends on two elements, the means of production and the people who work with them. From the united efforts of these human and mechanical agencies flow the material goods which are then sold by the enterprise as commodities. Thus enterprises depend on co-operation between people and the mechanical means of production. A common bond unites those who partake in the economic achievements of the enterprise. This consists of the entrepreneur (industrialist), the workers, and the means of production. To be sure the machines are but lifeless, yet have been created by an active human mind in conjunction with living human labour. The means of production represent capital in the form of mechanical power. Without it human labour could not be properly productive, nor could the means of production be of any use without human hands to make them work.

The much sought after ideal of a community of work requires a social structure which naturally suits its purpose. Such a development is greatly hindered by the materialistic, mechanical conception of industry as if it were but a mere combination of functional mechanical operations.

When an enterprise takes its rightful organic, social form, and is ready to attain the status of a true working-community, then the management, the workers, and the machinery will merge together into a social body, of which they would all be members. In every body, the organs have equal status, because none can exist and function without the others. The head is no more important than the heart, and vice versa, while the digestive organs are no more important than either, although without them head and heart would perish. So, in industrial enterprise, management, labour, and machinery are of equal importance. This is not the case in the capitalist economic organization with its purely materialistic structure. Here, the entrepreneur is socially set above the other factors which go towards production. This is because he has the monopoly of claims on the business profits. For the same reason, the owners of the machinery, standing on their rights of ownership, demand a superior position compared with the other two factors. Yet entrepreneur and owner of capital are often the same person, or have close ties through their common interests. They confront the workers as a dominating force. In the face of these despotic forces, the workers enlist the help of the Unions to obtain as powerful a position as possible for themselves, by higher wage-claims, demands for a voice in affairs, and disputes over their work.

From such *unnatural* strife among members which all desire to become centres of control, powerful socially disruptive forces have been introduced, as organizing powers, into the modern economic system. That this can happen is due to an economic policy which models itself on the workings of a *machine*, as such terms as 'market mechanism' and 'price mechanism' frankly reveal. The opposition of the workers who live and fight for their existence in this economic machine does indeed become less, as they gain more an equal footing of power with those who control the machine. But the harm done to personal labour morals, and its social consequences, remain unchanged or rather are worsened.

For an organic development of the enterprise and of the position the workers hold in it, there are certain social requirements. The co-operation of technical management, human labour, and mechanical efficiency, is achieved by the *functional solidarity* of these three productive factors. However, this functional solidarity goes hand in hand with a truly *social* solidarity. It binds the three functional elements into a working-community, which embraces the entrepreneur side by side with the people around him, the owner of the machinery, the workers, the clerks. Such a business-community, which is demanded by the very nature of industry, is made impossible when those three groups representing production are allowed to fall apart, and the entrepreneur is considered the centre and representative of the whole business. He alone becomes the symbol of the continual perseverance of enterprise, while the workers, and the owners of the means of production, if the latter are not identical with the entrepreneur but stand outside as temporary stockholders, count as only a vague and variable element in the enterprise.

If one fully realizes the unnatural, anti-social character of such a business system, there arises the social question of the shared responsibility of all who are connected with the business. This must be established, before the economic system and individual enterprises can be brought to order. It is not a question of solidarity among the workers themselves, nor of solidarity among the management, but of *solidarity between both parties*. They must build together a communal spirit, for the purpose of a proper unity between their different functions. There are many signs of steps in this direction. Meanwhile, however, the workers will only achieve a firmer footing in the business by force, by labour disputes and the demand for a voice in the decision-making process. But their real desires are distorted, because they are expressed indirectly through wage demands. This indirectness of the wage demands is the result of the fact that the workers have no legal claim to the machinery with which they work, and thus no claim to the material assets of the business. Marxism demands that the workers must overcome their separation from the means of production, by depriving the capitalists of them through nationalization, thus placing them under common ownership. But such a conception of ownership has no meaning for the worker, and does not bind him any closer to the processes of production. It merely overthrows the power of the entrepreneur and the capitalists, but replaces it with the far greater and more impersonal power of the State.

Marx is as helpful in his negative criticisms as he is unhelpful in his positive suggestions. He is quick to recognize any social injustice. He says, 'We ask how the strange situation comes about, that we see a group of buyers on the labour-market who are owners of premises, machinery, and raw materials, and a group of sellers who have nothing to sell except their ability, their strength and skill. And that the first group is constantly buying, to make a profit and enrich means of production, while the second is always selling, in order to earn a living. The answer is, that this is a result of the dissolution of the *original unity between the worker and his tools.*' This unity is similar to the organic solidarity of the factors of production. When the worker today fights for a voice in the business, and for the nationalization of the means of production, their real motive is the re-establishment of the original unity of the worker and his tools. This unity depends on the solution of two vital social problems which are still clamouring for settlement. One is the determination of a *socially just formation of income* for the worker. The other is the *relationship of the worker to the means of production* and to the business in which he works, and to its profits. It is these profits, however, at which the Trade Unions' wage claims are particularly aimed. When these problems are correctly solved, the labour-market, with its devastating effects on the economic system, can be abolished. Only thus can the way be opened for a real working-community, based on the commonly shared responsibility of all members for production.

A JUST INCOME STRUCTURE

In order to gain the right attitude to the problem of a just income structure, one must think of the economic concept in terms of general humanity. Every human being is born with the necessity of preserving and evolving his earthly existence. This is an undeniable human *right*. All human beings have an *equal* claim to this right. This right consists mainly in a claim to the material means of preservation and development. It is therefore of an economic nature. Because everyone has an equal fundamental right, it follows that the division of the national economic product must be subjected to the principle of *equality*. Certainly, this equality is subject to qualifications, but it must form the basic foundation of the income pyramid.

Obviously, the lowest layer of this pyramid must be no less than can support human life in a decently dignified fashion. This includes nourishment, clothing, dwelling, and the commodities required for the satisfaction of normal cultural needs, and also the expenses of transport. Now, this basic wage need not be kept at the minimum level, but depends on what the national economy can manage to produce in the various fields of living-requirements. It is therefore a question of producing goods in sufficient quantity for everyone to have his share. All luxury articles, products of a superior but not necessary nature, are not considered here. In this idea of working for others, in order also to make one's own share possible, we see the guiding principle of all economy.

Does the modern economic system take this social necessity into account? It cannot, since it is based on the philosophy of everyone caring only for himself. Today, every member of industry looks after himself, whether he be entrepreneur, capitalist, or worker. He is only interested in his income. He is not interested in the fact that a number of his fellow human beings have too little income, or perhaps none at all. He leaves the solution of the problem of these poor people's existence to the State, in other words, to the impersonal agency of the general public. The discontented and selfish attitude of people living on national assistance is well-known. It is a sign that the income structure is not economically or socially correct. This is the cause of the exploiting attitude of many recipients of surplus income towards the general public.

The wage structure, or income structure, is the direct concern of all who take part in the manufacture of produce to meet social needs. For the fair and realistic division of this produce, it is essential that the representatives of industry come to an understanding on the subject of the wage structure, which is a necessary complement to the price structure, and look at the situation *objectively*, so that they can see exactly where goods are most needed, and how to meet this need. Here, not only the needs for consumer goods and investment goods come into consideration, but also the needs of the State, of education and culture, and of the weaker members of the community. The money for all these goods which are not called for by industry itself must be found by industry, over and above its immediate needs. At present, these non-industrial needs are satisfied by the State, not by industry. The State taxes industry and wage-earners, to make up these payments. Through these financial commitments, the State has become overburdened with duties which drive it continually to the limits of its resources. A system which is at variance in its different business units, which cares only for itself, and aims at earning as much as possible on principle, cannot relieve the State of its overburdening responsibilities, for the support of culture, for unemployment, and for needy branches of industry. To relieve the State of some of these duties, industry must strive to overcome its isolating principle of competition, and transcending the narrow requirements of the market, arrive at a universal co-operation. Such co-operation is essential, for the understanding of the economy as a whole, and to meet social needs willingly, because of understanding, not because of desire for gain. Production ought to be regulated by an objective awareness which ascertains demand, and this does not mean only that demand which is backed by purchasing-power. It is therefore also necessary to establish a proper income-structure, to create the necessary purchasing-power. Steps in this direction can be seen in the recent formation of expert committees for working out a basis for an economically feasible wage structure. This is a beginning, although it takes into account only the income of the wage-earner, and does not yet come to grips with the social problem of the general income structure. The minimum income demanded by the principle of human equality should be decided by industrial experts, and be made practicable by the gradual adjustment of production.

In this way, a practical solution could be found to the problem of a socially fair income structure. Production would then be controlled by the knowledge of *need*, not by the profit interests of the individual company. Production and income would both correspond to need. The market policy of selfish gain would yield, when the income structure progressed side by side with the price structure.

The State's national budgeting today is an attempt in this direction. It tries to meet economic and social needs by supporting the universal market economy. But this method can never lead to that understanding of demand which, through the unceasing co-operation of all branches of industry, would achieve a productivity that would really meet demand. The responsibility belongs to industry itself, not to the government. Only industry can achieve the ideal of an economically just income structure. Its just distribution, however, would need the State's legal sanction. How such an associative system of economy might be put into practice is described in Rudolph Steiner's works on national economy, and in my own.

Thus, the minimum income level would be valid both socially and economically. Every income, wage, entrepreneur's salary, fixed income, would be built around this minimum. Thus, the principle of justice would be realized in the income structure.

However, production is generally not static, and the creation of capital, arising from the uncontrollable force of technical progress, leads to the difficult economic and social problems connected with that part of the social supply which *exceeds* the minimum, and which must still be put to a good economic and social use. Here arises the complication, that a certain part of production must consist not of consumer goods, but of investment goods, capital goods. This is the cause of the fight to increase wages for consumer purposes, at the expense of forming capital for investment purposes.

THE WORKERS' CLAIMS TO THE PROFITS

After the turn of the century, the system of *standard wages* was developed. This fixes payment at a certain rate, although this varies in different branches of industry. The standard wage is a sort of minimum wage, but has lately reached a level far higher than the essential living-wage. The Trade Unions attribute to expanding production the fact that they are continually fighting to increase this minimum wage. However, productivity does not progress equally in all branches of industry. There are companies which fix their own standards of payment, including the entrepreneur's salary. It must be remembered that all wages are consumer-income. Thus, the entrepreneur's salary really means only that part of his income which is to be used for consumer purposes. Now, many firms make an extra profit, over and above what they pay out in wages, while the normal profits alone should constitute the entrepreneur's salary. Yet these extra profits go automatically into the entrepreneur's pocket, or to the owner of the means of production, who is generally a shareholder. This shows a misconception of the idea of income, when profit exceeding the entrepreneur's salary is considered his property. This sort of transfer gives rise to unearned income. Two radically different causes underlie unearned income and real earnings. The economic origin of earned income is individual industrial achievement. Such income is equivalent in purchasing-power to the labour value of the consumer-goods offered on the market. If, however, sums of money made available by administrative or technical progress are transferred into private income, instead of going into the national economy, these sums are *unearned income*. Yet the law sanctions this. The workers, supported by the Unions, are now laying claim, in no uncertain manner, to these extra profits.

Division of business profits is managed in various ways. In general, division according to percentage has been adopted. This adds extra income to the standard wage. Voluntary bonuses are a milder form of this. The need to save part of the profits for investment purposes has led to *investment wages*, whereby the extra payment is not handed over in full, but some of it ploughed back into the business, while the workers are given shares for this amount. Such a policy is only attractive to the worker because it increases his income, in the shape of interest and similar compensations. But there is no doubt that he is bound by this procedure more firmly to the business, at least superficially.

However, none of these methods of dividing extra profits affords the correct social and economic solution. What right has the worker to lay claim to special profits arising from productivity, a boom, or the entrepreneur's strategy on the market? For none of these extra profits is originally due to the workers' achievement. The worker merely plays the part of an obstetrician, who does not produce the child, but only lends a hand in the final process. For this he receives his fee, but has no claim to the child. When the workers argue that physical work alone is productive, and any increase in productivity is due to them, they are wrong. Progress in production does not spring from an increased expenditure of physical labour, but from the creative mind which organizes the labour so that the same results can be achieved with less effort. No industrial machine is worth the invention, unless it saves human labour. Individual labour productivity depends on capital productivity and capital intensity. Therefore, an increase in wages should not depend on increased individual performance, since industrial and technical administration aims at *saving* human labour. From this point of view, the fight to shorten hours is entirely in accord with the proper development of the economy. But this is not so in the case of a shortage of labour. Such a shortage does not normally arise, but it can be caused by a sudden absorption of workers for non-industrial ends, or the departure of workers, or excessive economic expansion which outstrips the supply of workers.

It is therefore in general a mistake to correlate increased personal achievement with an increase in wages. However, if we turn from the causes of productivity to its results, we see that rising productivity means an increase of supply. More goods are produced with the same expenditure of labour. So that they can be bought, there must also be an increase of consumer-income. Here arises a great social problem. How shall the increased supply of goods be divided? The workers see the rising stock of goods as part of the entrepreneur's profits, and lay claim to as much as possible. With what right? The principle 'to each according to his achievement' leads nowhere. A different rule applies here. As progress in productivity is really due to the creative human mind, then it is valid to say that everything created by the human mind belongs to Mankind as a whole, although the investors of the productive machines may be granted a personal share of the profits of productivity. Industrial progress arising from the principle of division of labour, in particular, is not individually attributable. Humanity, or any social community, stand united in relation to the general supply, and the question is only, what share each individual can and should receive. This is not only an economic problem, but a social problem, above all a matter of common justice.

RIVAL CLAIMS ON CAPITAL

By 'capital', we mean here those surplus amounts which in business are called extra profits. From the point of view of the economy as a whole, however, they are new capital, or free capital. Various parties lay claim to this capital, some with justification. They thus compete for the entrepreneur's profits. First come the *entrepreneurs* and *capitalists*. They base their claims on their need for investment capital. Therefore they think it only right that the law has accorded them direct ownership of this surplus. Secondly comes the *State*, which obtains a sizeable portion of these profits by income tax and corporation taxes. Thirdly come the *workers*, who desire to increase their income. Fourth, however, should come another claimant, which does not realize its right to make a claim, although it has a better right than any of the others. For this claimant is the general cultural life. As we decided, all industrial progress is originally due to the creative human mind and spirit. By culture and education alone is the mind developed, and this development affects every sphere of life. Yet culture today is like a slumbering giant, unaware of its own strength. It would be more justified than all the rest in laying claim to the profits of productivity, in the knowledge that it is their original source. But culture today allows itself to be supported by the *State*. This is too great a responsibility for the State to cope with properly, so that culture always comes off badly, as far as finance is concerned.

But now the case is complicated by the fact that the entrepreneurs, who are creative in the fields of administration, technology, and market strategy, are themselves included among the representatives of culture. They represent that part of her which is not asleep. And as they are awake, and fully aware of their achievements, they lay *entire* claim to the profits. They look on it as a natural law that these should be added to their income. But thus a socially falsified situation is created. The entrepreneurs, in studiously ignoring the fact that they owe the development of their abilities to education, live in social blindness. They are mistaken in thinking that they alone should receive what is really a product of education, and in the creation of which they played only a final part. They are blind to the fact that they represent only the last link in the chain of causes which creates productivity. Only social ignorance could make them think they have the right to manage industry for the sole purpose of making the highest possible profits, and then requisitioning these profits for themselves. Against the injustice of this claim, the campaigns of the workers are basically aimed. The entrepreneurs should claim only a part, and should agree on a suitable portion being given directly to education and culture. This was done by the Zeiss Foundation.

Certainly, on grounds of their greater responsibilities, the entrepreneurs can justly lay claim to a higher income than the workers. But their salary itself comprises this higher payment. The workers must acknowledge this difference between their own wages and the entrepreneur's salary as entirely justified. They will do this when they can feel that the whole structure of income is just. They understand that their wages are based on their achievements, and the entrepreneur's salary is based on his special achievements. But they rebel when they see *additional* income being allotted to the entrepreneurs and capitalists, which does not represent either physical or mental achievement. The extra capital thus gained by the entrepreneurs is supposed to form the foundation for the necessary investments. This is their economic argument. But economic logic does not impress the workers, who think in terms of social logic. Even if the workers understand that the extra profits are not due, as Marxism claims, to their own achievements, their inborn sense of social justice will still prompt them to say, 'We know that you requisition the extra profits because you wish to use them for investment. But where is the guarantee that you actually use them for investment purposes? When we see the expensive way so many representatives of your class live, we get the impression that you are adding part of this capital, which you say is to be used for investment, to your salary, so as to be able to afford a luxurious way of life. And what is right for you must also be right for us. You transfer investment capital to your private income, so that it becomes consumer-capital. So why shouldn't we, too, get a share in the profits of the firm we work for, so as to increase *our* consumption?'

This argument removes all grounds for the arrogation of special profits by the entrepreneurs and capitalists. The worker feels this prerogative of the entrepreneur as an oppressive social contrast to his own living conditions.

The appropriation of capital produces a feeling of economic security in the entrepreneurs' superior social circle, which is completely lacking in the workers' lives. This security is further increased by the fact that the owner of the means of production has power at his disposal which at any time he can realize in cash, and thus in purchasing power, even if it means suspending production. But the worker is forbidden any relationship of ownership to the means of production with which he works, as well as to the profits they create. He feels this lack of security strongly, and today there is a movement to provide him with it, by giving him rights of ownership. These would consist of durable consumer goods, such as a house, or industrial security, such as shares, or other rights in the business.

II

Capital Ownership and the Sources of Income

THE ENTREPRENEUR AS TRUSTEE

All these campaigns to make the worker into a petty capitalist and co-entrepreneur are a grave mistake. The workers hail these movements only from their consumer-interests. They are quite indifferent to becoming capitalists or co-entrepreneurs. These machinations only serve to increase their egotism, and lead them further and further away from what they really want, the real *working-community* their socially oppressed natures need. So far, we have only the beginnings of such a business unity, in the form of a good working atmosphere. The first condition of a business-community is that it should oppose all who would requisition capital for themselves. But the solution to the workers' problem does not lie in turning them into miniature capitalists through financial ownership of the machinery, but rather in a reformation of the rights of ownership of capital. The capital due to the nation, represented by special business profits, must not be allowed to become the private possession of the entrepreneur. It gives the capitalists an arbitrary power. They may use the capital in a way which does not answer social and economic needs. To prevent this, a form of ownership must be found which will exercise a control over the power of the individual to dispose of capital, limiting his function to that of a *trustee*.

The personal, fallible element would thus be replaced by *objectivity*. This administrative form of ownership would also involve a time-limit. Thus, capital would remain in the possession of the entrepreneur only so long as he could put it to good use, economically and socially. When that was no longer possible, another trustee would take it over. Under these conditions, the right to bequeath such capital would also cease. An heir could only inherit in the faculty of a trustee.

That the existing forms of ownership are inadequate is shown by the following. When, in order to maintain investment funds, the industrialists take the convenient way of appropriating the whole of the capital created by the nation, and calling this 'private income', this arrogation is obviously no economic measure, but a wasteful subterfuge. It is squandering of capital, and often bad investment. It is therefore inevitable that powers are at work, trying hard to put an end to this appropriation. First, there is the *State*, which by means of income-tax, maximum rates, corporation taxes, and tax on yield of capital, succeeds in drawing back about half of the profits from the capitalists. Then there are the *workers* in the respective businesses, who press for part of the capital to be given to them, by profit-sharing or direct wage increases, and thus to be transferred to the consumer goods market. All these measures possess the character of a *compulsory expropriation*, which only partially prevents the unjustified amassing of private income. There is still no guarantee that the remainder will be used for investment purposes, as the entrepreneur claims. The State's method of getting back capital is a roundabout resort, made necessary by the inadequacy of market economy. The State is thus reduced to the necessity of supporting culture and education as best it can, and of subsidizing industry either by buying up surplus stock, or by artificially keeping the market prices down, or by making investments neglected by industry, or by managing enterprises of its own, for which industry is too selfish to take responsibility, such as the railways, some banks, national assistance, the national health service, etc.

When one considers what a huge proportion of the capital is taxed by the State, almost exclusively for non-industrial purposes, to pay civil servants, to finance culture, for military expenses, for pensions, etc., it is clear that the national capital cannot, in any case, be used only for investment purposes. If it were, an economic expansion of disastrous proportions would result. It is essential that a fixed portion of industrial profits should be directly transferred into consumer income, to become a demand for consumer goods.

In times of industrial decline, the question as to how much should be used for investment, and how much for consumer income, always arouses that monotonous controversy in which the workers demand an increase of consumer income, and the entrepreneurs an increase of capital expenditure on investments. The workers say, 'Consumption comes before investment', the entrepreneurs say the opposite, in order, they say, that the workers may be kept employed. The Unions argue that in a decline the demand is not adequate to absorb supply. Therefore, let incomes be raised, so that demand can increase. Against this, the entrepreneurs argue that they need more investment capital, in order to keep the workers busy, but that high wages absorb this capital. Both these arguments are right in their assumptions, so that a paradox seems to arise. This paradox is resolved on closer examination. An increased demand for investment goods results in more consumer income being formed in that particular field of industry, because more work is needed to produce them. Thus, the workers' demand for increased consumer income accords with the arguments for the need of increased investment. For whether the profits of production are turned directly into income, or invested, in either case consumer income is formed. The only difference is that in the second case, demand for consumer goods may be *delayed*. The decision as to whether income or investment shall be served depends on the *nature* of the supply which has accumulated, owing to advances in production. Here, economic logic demands a formation of consumer income to buy this increased supply. If the supply consists of consumer goods, it is a question of creating the corresponding consumer income. But if it consists of investment goods, investment capital should be formed, in order to create demand for these.

Thus, from the national formation of capital which corresponds to increased productivity, two streams of money diverge. One flows directly into the consumer goods market, the other to the investment goods market. This divergence can be turned into a convergence, if the capital is administered in such a way that the increased production of consumer goods is coupled with a corresponding expansion of consumer demand, while the practical needs of investment are met, though not allowing investment to become an end in itself. The solution of this central problem of administration leads to questions concerning the creation of capital.

THE NEUTRALIZATION OF CAPITAL

Let us confine our attention to the argument between consumer interests and investment interests, about the utilization and division of the capital of a country. The total amount appropriated by the entrepreneurs and capitalists far exceeds any possible investments that could be made. This shows how absurd it is, economically and socially, for the national capital to go into the possession of the industrialists. It makes a really objective discussion on the correct utilization of new capital impossible. For such a discussion to be impartial, all personal interests must be excluded. This can only be achieved by *neutralization* of the capital under discussion, so that it is not directly accessible to any party. It must be placed under the control of a neutral element, consisting of economic experts who have no personal interest in its utilization. They must have the co-operation of the industrialists, who have the practical experience, and know the facts. But where social justice is concerned in the turning of national capital into consumer income, the workers, the State, and the representatives of education and culture must also have their say. Culture will thus have an opportunity of making herself independent of the niggardly support of the State. She will remind industry that the whole national capital is originally due to her influence, and will claim a suitable portion, to come *directly* from industrial funds, sufficient to enable her to carry on with her work successfully, providing industry with new scientific knowledge, and thus creating fresh capital.

Neutralization would rescue capital from the clutches of the irrational egotists who would appropriate as much as possible without any thought of its economic consequences. They turn industry, which should be a social unity, into a battlefield, thus putting into practice Darwin's theory of the struggle for survival.

If all newly formed capital is privately owned no proper income formation can take place. Genuine income serves consumption and should not become private property. Only capital used for investment should claim ownership rights. Therefore, half the problem of extra profits consists of an unsolved question of *ownership*. After a neutral body of experts has taken over administration of the profits, part of them must be returned to the entrepreneur, strictly for investment purposes, so that his ownership is limited to the function of a trustee. Thus, it is no longer part of his private *income*. He would no longer be owner, but steward. By the institutions of neutralization and trusteeship, economic logic and social justice would be served. An objective control would also be exercised with regard to the incomes of the workers, and unjust profit-sharing, which cannot be given to all workers equally, would be abolished. Workers in businesses which cannot afford to pay them bonuses work just as hard as their fellows who have a share in profits to which they have not contributed by any special effort.

After the entrepreneur has been given stewardship over that part of the profits destined by the experts for investment, the rest is turned into *income*, in the form of donations to culture, etc., and subsidies to the State. However, the State being now relieved of many of its responsibilities, especially economic and cultural, would not need so much money as before. Finally, the remainder of the capital would go into the incomes of the general consumers, including the industrial workers. For the general public, new capital is a sign of cheaper and better living. But for the workers, it is a sign that they need not work so hard. But if working hours are actually shortened, the formation of new capital may be reduced.

However, if wage-increases and profit-sharing are still demanded, at the expense of the new capital, all these improvements will be made impossible. But the workers' wages policy arises from their struggle with the entrepreneurs and capitalists. Once the latter's usurpation of new capital was eliminated, these wage demands would no longer be necessary. The fair fixing of incomes would take their place. Also, profit-sharing might be replaced by something similar, but fairer. As the wages come out of the business profits, which are not established until the end of the financial year, the compatible wage paid weekly or monthly can be considered as only a premature withdrawal from the profits, and can be supplemented by later payments from the profits. But the factory does not reckon with the special profits of increased productivity, when calculating the normal wages. These profits must be booked separately in the accounts, to overcome this difficulty.

If the reader agrees with all these propositions for economic and social reform, he will ask, how can the neutralization of profits, their first requirement, be carried out? The answer is, that special social institutions are needed to guarantee objective utilization. These institutions may be on a large administrative scale, or they may be connected with individual businesses, like the Commonwealth which Scott Bader and Co. Ltd. have developed in their plastics factory. This is an independent commonwealth, to which the entire profits, remaining after payment of wages, are handed over. To this community belong the entrepreneur, the other directors, and all workers and employees, all of whom have a say in the business. The profits are disposed of in the following ways: some to the State, as taxes; some for investment; some for bonuses to the workers; some to culture; some to charity; and finally a voluntary donation to the district in which the enterprise is situated. The whole of the entrepreneur's capital has gradually been put into the commonwealth. If a sufficient number of entrepreneurs took a similar course, this system of dividing profits could become more methodical, as other attempts of this kind show, as we will see later. Here, everything depends on an understanding of the egotistic instincts that ruin industry, and the surmounting of them by moral will-power. Only by such power can a really social element of control be introduced into industry, freeing it from selfish interests. Enlightened entrepreneurs and industrialists should discuss appropriate ways of effecting an objective administration of capital. It is more than likely that they would decide on the institution of neutral societies for such administration.

THE RELATION OF CAPITAL NEUTRALIZATION TO A
JUST INCOME STRUCTURE

The neutralization of new capital is essential for the just determination of income. We have already mentioned the idea of a basic minimum income. Let us discuss some other factors determining the just division of capital, and the determination of income.

Here, the question arises as to how the social product is to be divided, when there are no profits due to increases in productivity. The workers in such a static industry must be brought to realize that they must work to cover not only their own needs, but also those of other sections of the community. If those employed in industry only needed to work for themselves, they would not need to work nearly so hard. But as it is, they must work much harder, for the following reasons : because of the needs of the State; because of the needs of culture, especially education; and because there are people incapable of work, the old, and the needy of all kinds, who must be cared for.

If such a static industry wishes to determine and regulate its demand for labour by human needs, this must bring some sort of movement into it. For example, if armaments in the range of £2,000,000,000 are ordered, the industrial workers must realize that because this order will take many workers away from manufacture of consumer goods, and also calls for the production of a vast quantity of unproductive articles, they will therefore either have to work harder, or relinquish a corresponding portion of their wages, either voluntarily or by taxing. Or let us imagine that a new consumer article is invented, such as a new type of television or car. If, due to the demand for this commodity, the workers claim higher wages, they are behaving unreasonably. The workers covering a demand must ask themselves, how much harder they must work in order to be able to afford the car, or television, for themselves. The tendency to work overtime is a step in this direction, though an impractical one.

Therefore, in a static industry, that is, one which shows no progress in productivity, the question is one of determining *how much* work is needed to provide a certain standard of living, and *how much more* work must therefore be done to provide a higher standard of living. If this is really understood, the workers will not make unreasonable claims. When they do, it is at the expense of other people, and this is anti-social. It means that wages must be increased regardless of the fact that there has been no increase in productivity, and this leads to a devaluation of purchasing-power, and a general higher cost of living, which affects not only the workers, but all other members of the community. Nevertheless the incomes so unjustifiably raised obtain a further advantage at the expense of all others since their wages are spent on only part of the goods whose prices they have helped to raise.

However, even an *economically* fair income structure, one which takes into account the laws of correspondence between the flow of supply and the financial cycle, will not provide for that *socially* fair division of produce, which alone can create social harmony in industry. To achieve this, not only the actual level of the standard of living must be taken into account, but also the parity between it and other standards of living. The advertizing industry, which today swallows up so much capital, arouses more and more demand, based less on necessity than on *social prestige*. When the worker sees the disparity between his own standard of living, although this already exceeds the necessary minimum, and that of the privileged social classes, he feels discontent and hostility towards these classes, not from *economic* distress, but through *social* comparison. Through advertising, people are constantly being told what they must possess, in order to be up to date. The way of life of the privileged classes is the model for the living-standards set by the advertising industry. This way of life eventually becomes a standard of personal worth. Therefore, social contentment depends not only on the individual's actual social level, but on the relationship of this to the social *norm*. The average living-standard of the worker today is about twice as high as before the war, but it still lags behind the accepted idea of the 'norm', however fantastic.

Such social rivalry, springing from an immature sense of self-awareness, no longer takes economic logic into account. The workers take no notice, when it is pointed out to them that excessive wage increases cause inflation. For the question is no longer one of economic security, but of *social rights*, the need for which is rooted in the fundamental instinct for justice. It is therefore inevitable that new capital in the form of productivity profits must let loose a war over their division. All the workers' campaigns today are aimed at seizing as much of these profits as possible, to prevent their going into the pockets of the privileged entrepreneurs and capitalists. These social battles, which threaten the economic system with serious shocks and losses, would be made unnecessary, if the profits were neutralized as suggested, in the businesses themselves. Thus, capital would no longer be arbitrarily controlled by the State, but would be administered by industry itself, co-operatively, by an independent system based on social and economic logic.

There is another problem of fair division, which arises in the case of a worker who has children to support. The young unmarried worker enjoys the highest standard of living possible among the working classes. If he marries, his living-standard does not alter, so long as his wife works too. But this all changes, when children arrive and the wife has to stop working. The social question is, how far should the wage system take into account these domestic difficulties? Naturally, the bringing up of a new generation calls for sacrifices on the part of the parents. Most parents later find these sacrifices to have been worth while. On the other hand, the rearing of the new generation is also the concern of humanity in general, if only from the point of view of the continuation of the human race. Therefore, the community should shoulder part of the burden in this field of responsibility. However large a part the public is willing to take in the children's upbringing, industry must produce everything the children need. Everyone must co-operate in this, whether he has children or not. The money equivalents of this increased productivity must be suitably divided among the various parties responsible for the children. These are the parents, their fellow-workers in the business, and the general public. Thus, the bringing up of children is another reason for the necessity of a fairly graded income structure.

It must be remembered, however, that part of the neutralized profits are to be used to finance education. This, coming directly from industry, without intervention of the State, will relieve the public of much of its responsiblity for the workers' children.

III

The Search for a New Social Concept of Labour Relations

SOLIDARITY BETWEEN ENTREPRENEUR AND WORKERS

To overcome industrial strife, a relationship of *solidarity* between the entrepreneur, as employer, and the workers is needed. It is not a question of solidarity among the employers themselves, or among the workers themselves. Solidarity *between the two parties* is essential, for they both represent opposite poles of production, management and performance. This mutual solidarity must express itself through co-operation in every enterprise. Today, a strained relationship exists between management and workers, on account of the social contrast, rooted in their different mental make-up. However, they do have something in common, that is, egotism and materialistic greed, which leave their mark on industrial labour.

Both parties must *combine* forces, to achieve the best possible production, and the fair division of the profits of their joint efforts. These two aims are interdependent. For their attainment, it is essential that work becomes separated from the wages motive. *Wage considerations* must not directly motivate *performance*. An engineer, controlling a machine, is guided by the technical laws governing the correct running of this machine, not by desire for gain. His need for payment is on a *social* plane, and may not interfere with the technical processes of his work. Harmony between labour and wages can only be produced by a reformation in labour relations.

In order to make work independent of the desire for gain, the worker must be drawn further into the business, and be more deeply involved in its affairs. Thus, he will not form an isolated component in the enterprise, but can give the best part of his individual personality to it, so that his work becomes motivated

30

by a sense of *responsibility*. This feeling of responsibility leads to a feeling of satisfaction. In work done in this spirit, the moral power of selflessness is prevalent, and this is essential to the realization of the ideal of human dignity, which is today people's principal social need.

However, for a system of labour relations which respects the dignity of the workers, a just wages structure is necessary. The workers must be able to feel satisfied with its fairness. Payment should no longer be looked upon as *wages*, but as part of the business profits, from which they are paid out. Payment should no longer be based on uniformity of achievement, and counted as expenses, against the business profits. It is surprising how little today people realize the unnaturalness of such a system of accounting, or see how socially untenable it is. Humanly speaking, all the employees of a business, including the entrepreneur, have a common right to the normal business profits. *Special* profits, as we have said, must be neutralized, to remove them from the selfish power of the individual. The socially right division of profits would have the effect of *increasing productivity*. This is because it would enable the worker to come into the business as a free individual, and do his work *willingly*, from a sense of *shared responsibility*, and not from the *compulsion* of having to earn *wages*. Under these conditions, entrepreneur, directors, and workers, all look on the business as their common support and through this sense of unity they are no longer opponents, but collaborators. If the workers feel the income structure to be fair, and that the entrepreneurs by their heavier burden of responsibility, are entitled to a higher income, then the main obstacle which now prevents them from devoting themselves whole-heartedly to the enterprise will have been surmounted. They will feel bound up with the business as a whole, and feel it to be the basis of their existence, and thus their work will benefit.

Under such conditions, the worker receives the *security* for which he longs. The human-social element binding him to all his fellows in the business, and the technical element binding him to the means of production, must, however, be of such a nature that the worker feels securely anchored in the business as a *sharer in responsibility*. The difficulty of achieving such a double bond is that today, in the West, people have reached such a stage of individuality that special demands are made on their initiative, which they might prefer to evade, through laziness. To overcome this *fear of responsibility*, the individual must be given the right social position, and permanent security. The ties binding the workers to the business must be made concrete through some sort of institution, such as was once a matter of course. Its re-establishment, under the altered conditions of today, is an urgent social need of our time.

OWNERSHIP OF THE MEANS OF PRODUCTION

When people lived in tight communities according to race or religion, they formed a unity, among themselves and in their relation to their means of production, which at that time consisted of arable soil and manual implements. They were not yet separated from one another by personal individuality, but remained members, all their lives, of the family and kindred in the community supporting them. Just so, the means of production were not separated by private ownership, but were the common possession of the community. It is to these conditions that the Socialists and the Communists really wish to return, when they aim at using the power of the *State* to weld the people into a collective whole, with, according to the Communists, renunciation of former family and religious ties. They would thus turn the means of production, nowadays mostly machinery, into an abstract, so-called communal possession, the representative owner being the State.

However, such a form of ownership cannot produce the mental and spiritual unity which once, in the times of tribal and kindred communities, gave common ownership a real meaning, and made it an expression of human unity. For then, the concept and its materialization were expressions of the community life of *families* or brotherhoods. Such ties can never be created by *nationalization*. Nationalization is fundamentally opposed to the principle of individual responsibility, to which modern man is suited. A *genuine* bond between the workers and the means of production must produce a real *working-community*. Such a community has the effect of anchoring the worker so deeply in the business, that he cannot help forming conceptions of ownership towards the machinery. Thus, it becomes '*his*' machinery he is working with. Such ownership, cannot, of course, involve unlimited rights of disposal, which might include sale. It must be a *trusteeship*, that is, utilization ownership. *All* members of the business must share equally in this utilization ownership. This ownership is neither directly nor indirectly a source of income, but gives all members a claim to utilization of the machinery, and a responsibility for this utilization. A firm bond thus grows between these trustees and the business, and gives them permanent security.

Such a form of ownership, in the framework of a genuine working-community, is therefore vital. It is a question of the modern renaissance of the original unity of the workers with their tools, which in olden times was taken for granted. The social, technical, and legal separation which in the course of time came about between the workers and their means of production was considered by Marx to be the chief fault of the modern economic system. This separation must be done away with.

The real working-community depends, therefore, on two special forms of ownership : utilization-ownership of the means of production that is ownership for actual use, and neutralized-ownership of the new capital formed by industry and represented by extra profits. Empty theorizing will lead nowhere. Our age demands the understanding and goodwill of the entrepreneurs, and the workers' willpower and capability for responsible cooperation. The entrepreneurs, above all, must discipline themselves, and summon up the strength to apply part of the effort that goes into their struggle for gain, for general social purposes. They will be rewarded by the increase in productivity. For the workers will be inspired to greater efforts, by the social atmosphere of the working-community. However, they too must contribute towards the creation of such a community in which they can transcend their selfish wage policy. To find what steps they themselves must take towards its creation, we must examine in detail the social techniques by which a working-community can be established.

THE PHYSICAL AND HUMAN POLARITIES WITHIN AN ENTERPRISE

We have established that the neutralization of ownership of new capital or extra profits is an essential condition for the creation of a working community, and that utilization-ownership of the means of production is a necessary result of such a community developed to its highest stage.

However, the details of the actual working-community itself, given such conditions, must be evolved by the two social partners, the workers and the management. By *partners*, I refer to their equality on the labour-market, an equality proved by the workers' right to payment.

The workers confront the individual entrepreneurs *collectively*. It is very important to remember that the workers always appear as a group, although little real unity is involved, but only a formal unity produced by the consciousness of their social position. Sometimes this unity is expressed through Trade Unions. The entrepreneurs, however, appear *singly*, as independent individuals. This individuality conforms with their function of leadership, which includes responsibility for the whole enterprise.

This difference between the entrepreneur and workers is due to the contrast between their different mental and spiritual make-up. This expresses itself in other differences; the quality of their talents, their spheres of responsibility, the very fact that one directs and the other executes. The entrepreneurs are concerned with the enterprise as a whole, through their awareness of responsibility for the economic goal of the business. They do not live for the present, but for the future of the enterprise. The workers are different. It is their nature to be concerned with the immediate present, their jobs and their daily needs. Yet they have the same fundamental human need for *community*.

In their attitude to life, there is therefore a characteristic contrast between the two types of people called to co-operate in business. Occasionally these differences are wiped away, especially when the workers become infected by the entrepreneur's desire for gain, and try to force their way into the entrepreneur's way of thought, as many Trade Union officials have succeeded in doing. On the other hand, many entrepreneurs have aspects of character which approach the mental make-up of the worker. All these nuances, however, do not belie the fact that there is a great difference between the two parties who are called upon to get on with each other. The clerk, who takes a sort of middle position between the two, inclines towards the entrepreneur in his general outlook, but in his concern for the enterprise, more towards the workers. However in the long run, he stands in the same social relationship towards the management as do the workers.

Technical considerations are also involved. The entrepreneur's ideas remain unfruitful, if he cannot find people to carry them out. And those capable of work cannot survive, if they are given no opportunity to work. The workers are really the suppliers of work, while the employers are the receivers, although the workers are generally seen in a *passive* light, as employees, and the employers in an *active* light. But this is because people are blinded in their judgment by the superior power of the employers. Thus, because the entrepreneur has rights over the means of production, he is looked upon as superior to the workers. This conception of labour relations is not appropriate today. Both parties are, in fact, seeking work. One seeks achievement, the other seeks to achieve. This difference in technical functions corresponds to the difference between the entrepreneur's mental and spiritual responsibility and the workers' physical responsibility. For production is material in its nature, although it does demand the individual conscientiousness and pride of the worker. The two parties were formerly called 'bourgeois' and 'proletariat', but this is no longer appropriate. However, the human difference still exists.

But these two powers in the industrial field must come to terms. From co-operative industrial powers, they have degenerated in two separate social classes, which are mutually hostile because of the contrast between them. Under these conditions, they can form only an abstract relationship in which everything human is eliminated. But fruitful co-operation in industry demands true human relationships.

THE OPERATION OF THE WORKING COMMUNITY

In the balance between the entrepreneur's sphere of individual responsibility, and the workers' sphere of collective responsibility, the basis of all industrial co-operation can be seen. Since the workers in a business are generally only *superficially* united, today, as fellow wage-earners, no working-community can be created among them. To form workers into an active social working-community, they themselves must undertake a commitment, responsibility for their work, not only individually, but jointly shouldered. Thus, all are collectively responsible for the completion of work done co-operatively. Today, the worker feels responsible for his job only out of wage interests, not interest in the

D

business, and not as a member of a responsible task force. A real working-community can only become possible, when the workers, as a single group, *guarantee* to the management all the work they are performing.

This grouping of workers in teams, although collective, must arise from the individual will of each member, and function through this. Of course, this does not mean that entrepreneurs may not affect the will of individuals, inducing them to form groups. This will sometimes be necessary, as some workers will always remain passive, and even indifferent.

Responsible groups of workers might be termed production-responsible work teams. To a certain extent, such teams were formed in Germany after the war. They were a promising beginning, but developed no further, as German industry, built up again under American influence, returned to its old forms of capitalistic market economy, and work once more became governed by desire for gain.

However, a responsible team, comprising the personnel of one business, cannot exist as an isolated group. Rather does the total sum of all such teams form the lowest stage of a working-community comprising all workers. The amalgamated production-responsible work teams would correspond, on a higher plane, to the existing Trade Unions.

Through the production-responsible work teams, the performing partner in industry would be brought into co-operation with the managing partner. In the team's acceptance of responsibility for perfecting all work according to the requirements of the management, this perfection is *guaranteed* by the team, and *achieved* with the help of the management. This is what is meant by co-operation. Now, the business is only the tool of the enterprise as a whole, but the responsible team forms a bridge between the enterprise and the business. The entrepreneur centres his duties in the business, and the enterprise draws its life from his initiative. The entrepreneur is responsible for the capital which supports the enterprise and the business, and for the final success of the whole. This responsibility also extends to the market's utilization of his products. The workers are not qualified for this high level of responsibility. They interfere in it today only when motivated by wage disputes. When these motives disappear, the workers will no longer need to interfere in the management of the enterprise, for which they are not cut out, and cannot take the responsibility. Their responsibility is confined exclusively to the business, to the work in which they must co-operate. This does not mean that workers cannot become entrepreneurs. Some workers today have the necessary ability.

The individual enterprise can become a constructive social force only through the form of a working community, and such a community can only become possible when the workers in a business can feel completely confident that the whole enterprise is being *objectively* administered. The main guarantee for this is the neutralization of new capital. Confidence in the directors, and recognition of the entrepreneur's heavier burden of responsibility, is made impossible unless the directors show that social attitude which can only arise when they no longer desire to appropriate the extra profits. The same selflessness is demanded from the workers. They, too, must be freed from wage considerations and do their work from a feeling of pride and a sense of responsibility. Thus, objective impartiality is required of both management and workers, for the creation of an impulse of responsibility among the workers, individually and as a whole, and for the development of this impulse into some form of responsible team.

When the entrepreneurs renounce their egotism, thus performing an act of social and economic reason, the extra business profits will cease to be a target of Trade Union wages campaigns. In the same way, the workers will lose their ambition to have a voice in the higher economic affairs of the enterprise. This voice would be transferred to the more general sphere of the social institutions formed to decide such questions as the satisfaction of demand, a fair income structure, and the utilization of new capital according to economic logic and social justice. For the socializing of labour relations calls for reformation of the economic system, especially the abolition of the all-pervading market philosophy. Our economy, which governs all its processes by the selfish concern for gain, can *never* become socialized.

The social problems of economy cannot be solved by any individual, still less by the State, whatever plans these may put forward. The responsibility lies with all who are occupied in industry. They must co-operate to produce the right sort of industrial transformation, in all fields of industry. For the reorganization of the economic system as a whole, the associative principle is needed.

This would operate through the mutual co-operation of the consumer, the entrepreneur, the workers, and the merchant. Rudolph Steiner has described this system and its practice.

To sketch briefly the ideal form of business, it must be brought about, as I have said, partly by the workers themselves, through their forming production-responsible work teams of their own volition. These teams, in order to be able to negotiate, would need a committee, which might be called a business council, which would exercise a controlling function.

The actual administration of production, and distribution of work, would still be the responsibility of the management, which is responsible for the central administration of the enterprise. Responsibility for the whole lies with the entrepreneur himself, who is in turn participating in the associative relationship. There are also the lesser responsibilities of the other directors. Then comes the responsibilities of the individual workers, in the field of performance, for which they are also jointly responsible, through the production-responsible work teams. The extent of the workers' responsibilities, which vary from company to company, is fairly similar for each worker. The main exceptions are the foreman and supervisor.

IV

The Workers' Responsibilities

THE SEPARATION OF WORK AND INCOME

It is the *extent* of individual responsibility which should chiefly determine the standard of payment. The wage-earner must realize this. Yet it is crucial that wages do not form the motive for achievement. Work must be done solely from a sense of pride and responsibility. The system of standard wages is a step in this direction. The Trade Unions' wage claims, too, operate independently of any consideration of the extent of work achieved. This, however, has the disadvantage of continually raising wages *on principle*. This aspiration is provoked by the entrepreneur's appropriation of new capital, in which the Trade Unions want the workers to share. The distribution of income has thus become a serious factor of disturbance of the economic system, and to labour morals.

On the other hand, it is only natural that the worker cannot give of his best, unless he knows that he is getting a *fair* and *sufficient* share of the national product. Only thus can work be kept separate from the wage motive. A fair income structure, however, cannot come about by leaving the matter to be argued out by the Trade Unions and employers. This approach has far too narrow a basis, and also involves the danger that the public may be exploited, either by the Unions or the employers.

The wage level must be fixed according to the individual degree of responsibility, and certain special social considerations, and must inevitably be limited by the extent of national productivity. But this fixed wage may vary slightly, according to the prosperity of a company. The varying and alterable dimensions of the turnover required in each business make impractical any fixing of the exact number of *hours* required by the job. The 8-hour day, the 45-hour week, the 5-day week, are all abstractions, brought about by labour conflicts. Real working-hours are fixed by the knowledge of the demand needing to be met, and by the needs of the enterprise. The fixed working-hours of today, supplemented by overtime, are an unscientific expedient. Of course, continually advancing technology is making the time required by a job shorter and shorter. In a real working-community, in which the workers really feel responsible for the work needing to be done, hours must be kept flexible. Nevertheless, increasing demand will sometimes need to be met by an adjustment in wages. A further reason for wage adjustment can arise from a boom, bringing profits which exceed expectation, or from a slump, when profits do not come up to expectation. In the case of extra profits, it is customary to grant extra pay, which, however, is deducted from the normal capital. This would no longer be possible, after neutralization of special profits.

However, in the case of profits being less than expected, the question arises as to how this will affect wages. Today, this is an undebatable question, since the workers' wage demands ignore the financial state of the business, and think only of higher wages. But in a real working-community, such questions must be decided by all the members. The workers in such a community would realize that businesses vary, in their profits, and therefore in their wage standards. As regards the entrepreneurs, differences in income are only to be expected, and have so far been no problem among them. This will still be the case when neutralization limits the entrepreneur's income to his salary. It would be absurd to standardize the entrepreneur's salary in every company.

The aims of the working-community are the firm anchoring of the worker in the enterprise, and his security for life, particularly through the bond of utilization-ownership of the means of production. For such ownership, only those workers can be considered who have won a firm position in the business. There will always be a certain percentage of drifters. These are usually those who are too young to have formed a clear attitude to their work and their aims in life. It is scarcely necessary to add that any member of a work team responsible for production or a working-community must be free to withdraw from the society. But in doing so he automatically loses his share in the ownership of the means of production.

For a long time now, there have been attempts to bind the workers more firmly to the business. The idea of permanent positions, recently developed in America under the name of 'seniority', is a step towards removal of the constant threat of dismissal hanging over the worker. Such a position is granted when a worker has been part of the enterprise for a certain length of time, say 15 years. This gives him security for life. But this security is not yet enough to urge the workers to a communal sense of responsibility, and thus unite them with the fortunes of the enterprise. They cannot be united with the business merely by individual workers being given a permanent position, in return for a commitment to perform adequately.

Only a joint responsibility for work, shared by the personnel as a whole, can give the workers a position equal to that of the entrepreneur, with equal rights. And only thus can the workers achieve real security.

PUTTING THIS SEPARATION INTO PRACTICE

The need for a genuine working-community, developed to its fullest stage, applies to all businesses, except the very small. The larger business sets its stamp on industry, and influences it generally. Smaller businesses have to conform. Most craft enterprises, however, have preserved a relatively independent existence. In such little businesses, consisting of about a dozen, or half a dozen workers, many contacts have been established, which themselves approximately in a way to a working-community. But they can never give permanent security, one of the main goals of the working-community. The division of responsibility between entrepreneur and staff, which is suited to the big business, is not suitable for the little business, where the entrepreneur often works at the same bench with his employees. Nor do quarrels arise over the entrepreneur's profits, as in large capital-forming companies, for the entrepreneurs in small businesses generally take only the salary due to them.

The idea of separating work from wage interests has recently been under consideration in certain circles. This isolation of wage interests would be attained by giving a social basis to labour relations instead of a wage basis, substituting pride in achievement in the place of anxiety for payment. Thus, the worker's *wage*, as such will disappear. Wages are the price demanded on the labour-market for the 'commodity', labour; but if the worker is admitted into the business as a person, and can feel himself a member of the community, he no longer stands in relation to the business profits as someone hostile or indifferent, who must unfortunately be paid out of these profits. In the working-community, part of the normal profits are paid out as wages in the course of the financial year, according to the dictates of higher social factors. But over and above these sums, and apart from the special profits representing capital due to society as a whole, other profits due to special achievement on the part of the workers find their way into the business proceeds. These sums are added to the normal wage. This is not division of profits, which is subject to other factors.

In the working-community, all its members, the entrepreneur and directors, as well as the workers and clerks, stand in an equal relationship towards the profits as a whole. This solidarity can never take the rudimentary, egotistic form of merely coming to an agreement over how the profits should be shared among the members themselves. This would be to ignore the capital due to society as a whole. This capital must be spent on investment, and to support cultural and social objectives.

Also, according to the spirit of the working community, wages and salaries should not be reckoned as expenses against revenue, but as shares in the earnings which are paid out in the course of the year, before the total amount of these earnings is known. After deduction of social and cultural allowances, wages and salaries should generally correspond to the profits. If the profits exceed the wages and salaries, then additional payments should be made. But this is not profit-sharing, which, properly understood, comes out of the funds free for capital formation, and is only justifiable if it takes society's needs into full account. Such a direct transference of new capital into consumer income may often be economically necessary, in order to provide sufficient purchasing power. But these complex economic problems cannot be thoroughly gone into here.

Our business here is to discuss the state of industry when the latter has been freed from the conflict that now tears it, thus making it possible in future for work to be done independently of wage interests. The need for this separation of payment and achievement is now beginning to be recognized. It can really only be put into proper practice in an economic system which is correctly administered from a *social* point of view. And until an effort *is* made to put it into practice, the economic system will continue to be socially incorrect. If it were correct, its members would work willingly, because it is generally man's nature to work willingly. But as members of a working-community, and of an associative economic system, they would be given a motive for working higher than that of personal gain.

A timely reformation of the concept of ownership, and a fair income structure, will put an end to wages resulting from dependency of the worker upon the labour market. But the separation of work from wage interest is the first condition for the realization of freedom in labour, for social harmony, and for the humanisation of industry. These three goals are worth working for, and if need be, fighting for.

V

Trade Unions and a New Social Order

In recent years, during which labour disputes have waged incessantly throughout the West, disturbing living conditions, the question of the function and responsibilities of the Trade Unions has been urgently raised. On this subject, valid conclusions can only be drawn if these responsibilities are considered in the context of a new industrial order. For what the Unions are really trying to express, especially in their struggles to gain a voice in business affairs, is, in fact, some sort of new social order.

THE SOCIAL UNIFICATION OF THE WORKERS

As I have said, the workers' production-responsible teams must not exist as isolated unities, but be united in wider confederations. Workers in similar types of industry face similar or identical problems. This has resulted in many Trade Unions forming alliances, as in the British Trade Unions Congress. In the case of forming such alliances among communities of achievement, two different principles would hold good, the *confederative* and the *centralized*. The two principles might complement one another. First let us examine how a team responsible for production can be called into being.

The necessary initiative can awake of its own accord in an enterprise. It may come from an enlightened entrepreneur, or from leading lights among the workers themselves. But the incentives coming from either of these two parties must be met half-way. One alone cannot succeed, without co-operation from the other side. But if real working-communities can be developed in a sufficient number of businesses, then the workers' inherent social instincts will quickly assert themselves, and they will find so many questions to discuss that their individual communities of achievement will establish relations with others, to decide these

44

mutual problems. The principle of *confederation* would here be operative.

But there are other points to be considered. To bring about neutralization of capital, and a fair income structure, essential conditions for the establishment of a working-community, a higher level of social awareness is needed. This can be awakened only by a general cultural and educational campaign. The convictions of writers and speakers, based on scientific fact, must be made to infiltrate more and more to the general public. Only thus can the impulse towards a new social order affect the masses. Any advanced social step taken by an individual company must remain an isolated improvement. It cannot alter the general structure of industry.

It would be an enormous help, in the development of work teams responsible for production, if the leading lights among the workers can become convinced of the need for all these changes. If their awareness were once aroused, they would have an educative effect on the whole working body. They would develop the necessary awareness in the workers, and awake in them a desire for a higher social order, and show him the right way to achieve this.

Thus it will be seen that workers would sometimes form groups from a mutual impulse, and sometimes through the instigation of a leader. The latter principle might be called centralized. The reason for occurrence of both these methods is that in the West, modern man has already reached a high state of individuality, but has yet to develop it further. For this alone can prevent the rise of a tyrannical central organization which would dictate to its members, or bully them about what they should think and how they should act. The freedom of the individual is a source of power transcending all other powers of organization, and without which the new, humanized industrial societies cannot arise. In these societies, the individual will feel like a human being, not a downtrodden payee, or a sort of untouchable, although he does indeed belong to a special class of people. In a system so naturally and harmoniously ordered, the Trade Unions will have to discard the warlike role they have taken on, through the fault of the labour-market, for they will be occupied with other functions. Their structure will have to undergo a revolution.

INDUSTRIAL DEMOCRACY AND NATIONALIZATION, AS
TRADE UNION GOALS

So far, we have dealt only with the Unions' role on the labour-market. But the extent of their influence is more far-reaching than this. Lujo Brentano, who was the first to fully grasp their importance, realized that they tended to have an integrating effect on the worker's personality, and endeavoured to comprehend him as a whole. This aspiration still exists, as is shown by the broad cultural aims of the Unions. They have set aside funds, to enable promising young workers to take scholarships and attend full-time courses at technical colleges and Universities. However, we will not go into this aspect of the Unions here. Let us confine our attention to the functions which, as representatives of the workers, they carry out in the organization of industry, functions which are necessitated and conditioned solely by the labour-market.

The main problem of labour, as I have said, is how to incorporate workpeople in the industrial system according to *economic* and *social* laws, and how to achieve the right sort of co-operation between management and workers. Obviously, and this is shown by the very existence of Trade Unions, the position of the workers in the system must be one of *solidarity*, for *social* reasons, even when it is no longer a question of their forming an alliance against the entrepreneurs and employers. Rather it is a question of the need for the workers to feel united in responsibility for their work, and the need for a fair and sensible wages structure. These vital goals cannot be achieved by a number of separate, isolated agreements but only by the social co-operation of all and sundry. Without such co-operation, too, working-communities cannot be formed.

Today, the Trade Union is only *in part* an expression of the workers' solidarity. As an element of the labour-market, and representative of its militant tactics, the Union naturally has no interest in the formation of working communities which constitute a higher synthesis than the Trade Union, because they are formed by the co-operation of the workers with the entrepreneurs, not just the workers with each other. In the place of these real, social unions, the Trade Unions substitute demands for *participa-*

tion in authority. The militant nature of such participation is due to the situation of the labour-market. Its aim is to develop resistance against the entrepreneur's power, and his abuse of it. They demand that the workers in large enterprises shall be represented on the board of directors and in the management, and shall be on an absolutely equal footing with the other members of these.

By such methods, they wish to gain industrial *democracy.* Behind the workers' demands for equal participation in every sphere of industry, lies the conviction that a truly democratic system will not be possible until the workers, as citizens, have not only a voice in the government of the State, but also a direct influence on industry. This influence would affect the factory, the enterprise, industry, and the economy as a whole. It aims at weakening the power of the biased judgment of the entrepreneurs and directors, and at revolutionizing the whole industrial system. They believe that industrial reform can only be brought about by *democracy,* and that democracy can only come through *participation.*

Now, a new industrial order worthy of the name must be brought about by adequate social methods. Only through such methods can the economic system attain the form necessary today. The idea that economic reform can be achieved by the *political* principle of democracy is based on an inadmissible transference of the social methods which are suited to the *political* system, to the *economic* system. This social method consists of the establishment of the will of the people, by a majority vote. Democracy is a political, not an economic concept. The specifically economic problems in industry, touching on the division and the nature of the product, the utilization of labour and capital, the distribution of raw materials, etc., cannot be solved by majority decisions or voting. They can only be dealt with by those who possess the *technical knowledge.* The workers are *not* specialists in this field. Only in questions which touch on one's instinctive awareness of justice, such as the question of power, and the division of profits, does *everyone* have the necessary knowledge. For such things *can* be decided democratically.

The most important element of any State is its social power, which exists to uphold human rights, in all human relations, therefore in industry too. The State must intervene when human rights are abused in industry. This does not mean that industry should be *nationalized*, and the State itself take over full responsibility. Only if the representatives of industry do not fulfil their duties properly themselves does nationalization become unavoidable. In a system where those occupied in industry pursue only their own private interests, production cannot meet true human demand, fair prices cannot be established, capital cannot be injected where it is really needed, and workers cannot be used properly. This means that the State is more or less forced to take responsibility for industry. In this way, a political method alien to industry creeps in. In the movement towards democratic ideas in industry there is some justice, but only in so far as concerns the abuse of human dignity and human rights. The social system appropriate to industry cannot come directly from the State, but only from the initiative of those in industry themselves. But when questions of justice do arise in industry, especially over the wages structure, the State must interfere. Such justifiable interference is today prevented by the policy of the labour-market, which bases the workers' payment on his achievement as though pricing a commodity. Thus, the national produce cannot be fairly divided. Justice is not a market concept, but a humane moral principle. Workers have always felt that the profits they have helped to earn are divided unjustly. From this point of view, political control of industrial power seems reasonable. But the fundamental principle must not be lost sight of. Among free people, fair shares should be gained by *mutual agreement*. Not until this is proved a failure, will the general public have to use the State to effect what it believes to be right.

Since in capitalistic industry the income structure is by no means based on the principle of just shares, but, as regards the workers, on market policy, and as regards the entrepreneurs, on their power over capital, the Trade Unions therefore feel they have good reason to attack the capitalists' power over resources. On the one hand, they use the political instruments of State-control and nationalization, on the other, the workers' policy of participation in affairs. Thus, industry has been turned into a battlefield, on which might fights against might. On this field, there are victor and vanquished, sovereign and subject. In order to break the power of the victor, the Unions make demands which are particularly levelled at concentrated power. Thus, they demand participation of the workers and Unions in all affairs, the revolutionizing of the enterprise concept, control of monopolies and syndicates, increased competition through public enterprise, the development of public enterprise, and the nationalization of key industries.

The elimination of *social tensions* in industry is, therefore, one of the main concerns of the Trade Unions. But besides this, they pursue aims which are directed at the actual *economic structure* of industry. In this, they are motivated by the functional flaws in the market economy. They can see that the price situation is hopelessly disorganized. They see bad investments, or failure to invest, the result of selfish private interest or of monopolizing. But they have no constructive ideas as to what they should really do to achieve a true new industrial order. They are still under the spell of the market, which, with the State's help, they wish to uphold. They demand an economic programme, they want the State to encourage investments, they demand full employment, steady industrial expansion, and stable currency values. They attach great importance to competition and planning.

Their ideas are completely lacking in originality, especially as regards their idea of a new industrial-social order. But the real problematic nature of their policy lies in their attempts at breaking private monopolistic power in industry, by the power of the State and the organization of workers. With these weapons they mean to destroy, neutralize, or reform private power. They want the State to control private power by extensive nationalization. Also, they want the workers to intervene in industrial affairs, on every plane. It is clear that this *soi-disant* industrial-democratic policy is not *positively* founded on industry itself, but is only *negatively* provoked by the anti-social philosophy of the industrialists.

When political democracy was established by the French Revolution, it was said that 'The power of the State comes from the people.' If we transfer this maxim to the industrial field, it cannot be said that industrial power comes from the people. It is held either by the entrepreneurs, or by the workers, or by the State. Any one of these three powers is a *social impossibility*, according to the true nature of industry and economics. For in industry, it is *never* a question of power, but of productivity and social collaboration, so that a co-operative production of goods can be made to meet demand. Positions of power have no place

in a system controlled by co-operation. Partial or total nationalization, and so-called industrial democracy are defensive measures
against social irregularities and economic errors in industry. They
have no *positive* bearing on the correct structure of industry, and
the words 'new order' cannot be applied to them.

If the Unions' demands were granted, what would be the result?
Industry would, to a great extent, take on the form of public
industry, and much of private capitalism would become State
capitalism. Such a compromise still does not lead to a new social
and economic order. Certainly, labour would still not be subjected to that compulsion which *Communistic* economic planning,
or dictation, exercises over it. And power over capital would
indeed be taken out of private hands, partly at least. This would
undoubtedly be a social step forwards, provided that it could be
carried out successfully. But whether it were also an economic
improvement, would depend on the utilization of the capital being
such as the real economic *experts* would recommend. Politicians
and civil servants do not come under the heading of economic
experts. The errors in Communist planning are sufficient proof
of this. But neither are the workers experts on economic procedure.
They do not have the knowledge, and are in no position to take
responsibility for the consequences of any blunder. They are
experts on their own *work*, and on the nature of the *social* conditions under which they would like to do this work, and on all
general questions of social relations. Therefore their demands for
participation in all spheres of industry are mistaken. They would
be exceeding their qualifications, provoked to this by the present
system with its dogmatic principle of universal markets, which
allows the final decisions for the technical control of economy to
rest with people who have only their own interests at heart.

The Unions' demands for a new order of the enterprise are
a very promising sign, and agree in their general wording with
my own suggestions regarding the working-community and
communal enterprise. But the Unions' conception differs fundamentally from the idea of true social co-operation between
management and workers. They wish to apply the abstract
principle of democracy to the individual enterprise. According
to this principle, the workers would mix with the management,
and have an equal voice in its decisions. On the board of directors,
the representatives of the capitalists, public interests, and the

workers, would all have equal rights. As a campaign against the misuse of power, these demands may be justified, but they are useless as a means of social reconstruction, and their methods are quite wrong.

Thus we see that these demands of the Trade Unions do not have any social originality, or any future. One cannot hope to deal with the harm caused by an anti-social system by attacking only its obvious symptoms, but allowing its underlying causes to persist. From this situation industry can be freed only by the alteration of its basic principles, by confining the anti-social market mechanism within narrow bounds, and replacing it with social institutions which transform the enterprise into a communal unit. The worker never really loses his longing for a true social transformation. The renunciation of his deepest instincts has degraded him to the level of a wage-grabber, who is not interested in industry, or even in his Trade Union. This fact ought to show the Unions where their real duties lie, if they wish to take the initiative in bringing about a timely new social order in industry. These duties would necessitate an alteration in their structure, which could enormously increase their efficiency.

THE TRUE RESPONSIBILITIES OF THE TRADE UNIONS

To put an end to the individual abuse of industrial power, an attack must be made on the foundations of such power. And this means that people must adopt a different conception of the nature of capital and the lawful ownership of it. Such an attitude, resulting in the neutralization of capital, would answer the deepest social longings of the worker. In his heart, he does not really want the continual fight for higher wages, nor to work as little as possible. What he wants is a place in Society befitting his dignity as a free man. When the workers gain this place, they will give of their best, of their own free will. But if they have to work for a system in which a host of egotists pursue their own selfish interests, the workers' natural instinct for responsible co-operation becomes dormant. But this sense of responsibility, which alone can make a person really free, must be awoken and developed, if the workers are to take an *active* part in the establishment of true social reform in industry.

The phrase 'human dignity' has, indeed, become a *cliché*. One

E

must have a personal understanding of the nature of this dignity, before one can understand the deeper problems of the workers. Human dignity does not always have the same meaning, in different ages, and among different races. The modern Central European feels he is in possession of his dignity only when he can see himself in his true character, not fallen into a state of passivity induced by fear of insecurity, concerned only to get by as comfortably as possible, with the minimum of trouble. Human dignity is based on two fundamental principles. One is the *sense of individuality*, which according to Goethe is man's most precious possession. It is only experienced, however, when a person plucks up the courage to take the plunge towards full *responsibility* for his own life, and thus accepts the duties which incidentally devolve upon him, and when he also makes those *moral efforts* which strengthen and develop his individual personality. The second principle of human dignity does not depend on him alone, but on the attitude of other people towards him.

Human co-operation is therefore indispensable to human dignity. This co-operation must not be such as would prevent the individual from taking responsibility for his own life, and making use of all his talents, both for himself and for other people. But he can only do this if he lives under conditions which are socially ordered in every way. An anti-social environment and working-atmosphere cripple the individual's natural impulses, and stifle his willingness to take on responsibilities. Co-operation is a force which creates a space in which the individual can feel free. But this space is not a vacuum, and he is no longer driven back on his own mental and spiritual resources, by indifference and covetousness on the part of his neighbour. He can turn to his fellows, open his mind to them, and work for them. He cannot do this under the present anti-social conditions.

In a correct system, the workers could take full responsibility for that sphere of industry which consists of *performance*. As we have said, their capacity for responsibility does not include the sphere of management. Their responsibility for achievement would be communal, and thus they would form social groups, and, at length, take on as a whole the character of an independent social element in industry, with definite rights and duties. The social unity of the workers must be constituted through Trade Unions, but these must not be the authoritative organizations they are today. They must be mutual alliances, in which the industrial and social instincts of the workers are expressed—'democratically', if you like.

In the United States, there are Trade Unions which have so disciplined their members, that they can afford to guarantee to the entrepreneurs, with whom they have an understanding regarding labour conditions, that their members will do good work. This is possible, even under the conditions of the labour-market. The production responsible work teams which arose in Germany after the war are a similar case. They took co-operatively the responsibility for the achievement of a fixed work load, which they did punctually and conscientiously without control by the employer, though their motive was egotistic wage interest. Such communities could again arise, but on a higher plane, in a system which had overthrown the labour-market. Here, teams responsible for production would not be isolated social organizations, but components of a higher Trade-Union organization, whose duty it would be to supervise labour relations in these communities, and co-ordinate the teams with industry as a whole. Because of the differences between various branches of industry, there will still have to be different Trade Unions. But the main thing is that the initiative of the individual worker will be called upon, not only for specific achievements, but to form the lower and higher forms of social organization which will all help to support the organization finally responsible for all work. At present, the Trade Unions hardly ever find support from below, on account of their members' *passivity*. Responsibility would change this passivity into activity, which would greatly strengthen the Trade Unions.

Now let us imagine that the Trade Unions had taken over their rightful social functions, co-operatively representing the workers, in the sense of taking responsibility for the workers' performance. They would also have to be directly active, in order to ensure that the payment for performance was correctly graded. This twofold function of the Unions, responsibility for work, and supervision of wages, would necessitate that *all* workers belonged to Unions. Anyone who did not want to would suffer all the social and material disadvantages resulting from his non-participation. He would be an outsider, and this would contradict the communal spirit of labour.

It is an inveterate evil of the traditional structure of the Trade

Unions, that in order to exist they must struggle to recruit members, and to make membership appear in the most attractive light. They are therefore under constant compulsion to prove the necessity of their existence. They have to institute periodic proceedings for increased wages and shorter hours. By doing this, they are appealing to the *egotistic* interests of the workers. Thus, they never appeal to the *social ideals* dormant in the workers. They cannot, for they do not consider it their duty to further such ideals, and have no clear picture of the practical realization of these ideals. They therefore wish to persevere in their war for higher wages and less work. To these aims they owe their birth, a hundred years ago. But then, those aims were justified by the conditions of the time, as they are always justified when there is capitalistic exploitation of labour.

Today, there are signs of a move to overcome this unfortunate situation of the Unions. Thus, for example, there is an increasingly strong movement to adapt the wage structure to economic resources. From this, it is only a step to the subjection of the workers' achievements, on which these resources are based, to technical control by the Trade Unions. This could be the beginning of the Unions' communal responsibility for performance. From this point of view, it becomes reasonable for the Unions to demand a 'solidarity subscription' from non-members who share in the advantages provided by the Unions.

CO-OPERATION BETWEEN TRADE UNIONS AND WORKING-COMMUNITIES

The more we are persuaded that this sort of a new industrial order must be brought about, the more we may doubt whether this is possible, in face of the firmly established structure of market economy today, and the equally established self-interest of its members. If the method of *revolution* were chosen, of course, everything would be possible. But revolutions are negative, only serving to overthrow existing conditions. When this has been done, it is by no mean certain that a *better* order will be established. Revolutionaries are generally better at destroying systems than creating new ones. We must therefore confine our attention to the *evolutionary* possibilities of a new order. Any social reform which is to be evolved from existing conditions, to be comprehensive, must be instigated by the workers and their Unions. For in the workers, the instinct for community is especially immanent. In fact, they possess the moral power which underlies all social co-operation, reverence for life, transcending all material interests.

Therefore, the Unions must make the first move in the direction of a new order, but this must be seconded by the joint support of the workers, who with the co-operation of the entrepreneurs must form working-communities. If these communities were organized as I have previously suggested, if they only settled for a compromise, as I will explain later, they would form the germs of that order for which industry is clamouring. This reorganization of the whole economic system, born of the desire of the workers themselves, would automatically lead to the production responsible work teams forming alliances through their representatives, the works councils, and, in separate branches of industry, organizing themselves as lower units of the Trade Unions, or as shop committees. Through such amalgamations, the workers would give active support from below, to the main Trade Union organizations, which would exercise their extensive powers from above. It is the responsibility of the Trade Unions to introduce the workers' spirit of social co-operation into the smaller bodies of the working communities, as well as into the greater central organizations. The workers' instinct for social co-operation will eventually extend to the wage structure itself. The way in which this will happen will depend upon particular circumstances.

It should be remembered that the social organization described here does not apply to the smallest businesses, or to crafts, small scale retail businesses, or, of course, agriculture.

I repeat once more that the new industrial order depends, for one thing, on the reform of the concept of ownership. Not until we have succeeded in eliminating individual power based on private ownership of capital, power which is a continual source of disturbance to the economic system, and has stirred up the lasting war of the workers for a share in industrial profits, not till then will the Unions be free to take on their real responsibilities. Then Utopia will no longer seem a pipe-dream, when the Unions accept the final responsibility for performance, and as representatives of the new labour morals take on the special function of initiating new ways in industry. When the barriers of private capital ownership are overthrown, or at least kept within bounds, the way will be open for the Trade Unions to exercise their true functions in the field of incomes. The fair and practicable participation of the workers in the national product, or in business profits, can only be decided by people with the highest sense of social responsibility. Here, this would involve consideration of the fact that industry must support not only the workers, but their families, the unemployable, the pensioners, not to mention the State, and education and culture. In the business, such a correct division of new capital can only approximately be achieved. But there is the danger that entrepreneur and workers may divide the profits without regard to the financial needs of the rest of the public.

It will therefore be necessary to find out what is the sum total of the social supply available for consumption, and then to decide what should go to each person as his economic and cultural minimum. It can then be decided how high to set the standard wage, and how far this should be considered binding. Parity between incomes reflects the social character of labour, and is a sign of justice, despite all the graduations which occur in different situations. From this point of view, the policy of wage-tariff agreements conform to social ideals. But negotiations over a suitable wages structure must be carried on in the greater context of the correct utilization of the national product. In these discussions, not only the Unions should take part, but also representatives of the other income recipients: civil servants, pensioners, and those culturally active. In this way, wage claims could be made which were economically realistic and socially fair. Then there would no longer be any reason for the Unions to intervene in business management, or to demand the nationalization of the means of production. If their leaders can rise above the dogma of selfish market economy, and above all, gain a true understanding of the nature of society as a whole, then they can systematically co-operate towards a real industrial reformation, or perhaps bring it about themselves.

If the Union leaders were to apply their special economic and social insight to the present labour conditions, they would find themselves faced with a special *cultural* responsibility towards the workers. It would become their chief concern to educate their members in the new way of thought, and to prepare them to take over their rightful industrial responsibilities.

Today, there are already attempts to bring about a new concept of ownership. These attempts are made by individual entrepreneurs, who have understood the new spirit of the times. What they have done in this direction is only a beginning. But such beginnings are as valuable as the achievements of any pioneers. They pave the way for practical compromises. I will go on to speak of these attempts, for by them the social ideals described here are brought nearer.

VI

Stages in the Constitution of the Enterprise

The communal enterprise we described expresses a social ideal. The recent use of similar terms, to describe any social partnership formed in business to uphold the accepted system, has been rejected by many Union leaders. It is true, also that the expression has a rather sentimental flavour, a 'cosy' sound. But any element of 'cosiness', such as exists in the patriarchal concept of business, with its 'father-figure', is entirely lacking in the concept we are dealing with here. The 'human' element in it consists of an *objective social attitude*, a disinterested public spirit, as Rudolf Steiner calls it. This is, indeed, deeply rooted in humanity, that is, in the belief that every individual has the right to freedom. And *Personal* human relations may *arise* from the business-community or even play a part in its creation. Certainly, what today we call a good working atmosphere is an essential condition for the formation of a communal enterprise. But mutual respect, interest in the business, and a sense of justice in wage relations are already forming a good atmosphere in some businesses, yet without producing a working community. However, this atmosphere helps to develop a social conception of business. This conception may be realized in different ways, which may have more or less far-reaching social effects. Besides the final stage, the perfect community, there are also preliminary stages, which serve to bridge the way towards the real thing. These intermediate stages throw a special light on industrial problems.

I will go on to describe all these lower or higher stages of co-operation, under the general heading of social conceptions of business. Note, by the way, that here, the word 'business' usually refers to enterprise. Bearing this in mind, we can go on to say that the social conception of business may be realized in three stages:

1. Lowest stage: the business partnership.
2. Intermediate stage: social business integration.
3. Final stage: business association, the true working-community.

Compared with the last stage, the first two are only compromises. Naturally, the higher stages generally include the elements of the lower. It also follows that each stage may appear in different variations and transitions, and therefore cannot be dogmatically classified. Especially the transition between a social integration and a full-fledged associative enterprise is a fluid one. For the latter no example can as yet be given, but integration is a preliminary to it. So it is understandable that the term 'association' is sometimes applied to business integration.

THE COMMERCIAL CONCEPTION OF THE ENTERPRISE

The opposite of the social conception of business, in its various stages, is the commercial concept, which is expressed by the market economy. The labour-market and the dependency of wage earners upon an employer are results of it. So is the attitude that payment can be the only motive for work. The main feature of this mercenary conception is the invariable seizure of material advantages, not only in the exchange of wares for money, but also in the exchange of work for money. Everywhere, rival materialistic interests compete. The entrepreneurs and capitalists, supported by the accepted laws of ownership, fight to get the business into their own hands, for their own ends. This tends in the direction of absolute autocracy. The workers oppose this, and claim increasingly large shares of the profits, and a cutting down of work. Out of all this, a thoroughly anti-social situation arises. In particular, the workers increase their struggle for greater participation in the business management. It has become one of the principal bones of contention between the workers and the entrepreneurs. The latter maintain that they have an exclusive capacity for management, and are supported in this by the existing forms of ownership.

But in proportion as the workers are motivated by mercenary

interests in their demands for participation, so do they feel more and more drawn towards a social conception of business. True participation by the workers can only come about through a social conception of the enterprise. Otherwise, if the workers bring it about by force, the anti-social nature of business today will not be altered. It will still be mercenary, and still represent a battlefield on which workers and entrepreneurs pit their strength against each other. This will be so, even if their squabbles are transferred to a wider industrial field, for instance, the question of an economically reasonable wage structure. No truly social relations would result, but only technical relations, like those between the contracting parties of a bill of exchange. This does not mean, of course, that in spite of this human relations cannot be established, sufficient to generate a good working atmosphere. But this is not enough to bring about a truly social structure of the enterprise.

THE BUSINESS PARTNERSHIP—GERT SPINDLER AND SHARED-ENTERPRISE

A typical example of the business partnership is the textile factory of Gert Spindler in Hilden. Spindler is an entrepreneur who understands social problems. He saw that the workers were groping towards maturity as individuals, and could no longer be used as passive tools. He is ready to sacrifice part of his traditional rights as entrepreneur to this idea. It does not hurt his self-respect to sit down with his workers, talk to them about the aims of the business, and concede them the right to participate in discussions and decisions on most technical points of administration and performance. Again and again, in his book *Shared Enterprise*, he repeats that the worker wants to be recognized as an individual, and that the business must be the first to do this. He knows from experience that the power of capital and its implacable philosophy of gain prevents the worker from developing his personality, and has driven him into class-warfare. Spindler wishes to remove the cause of this war. To do this, the entrepreneur must undertake new, greater, social responsibilities. It will no longer do for him to look on the business as something which serves only his private interests. He must understand that he has a socially educative responsibility towards the workers.

It is his duty to awaken and develop a sense of responsibility in the worker. To do this, he must make him an equal partner in the business. Partner means sharer. Under the existing conditions, the worker has become quite passive and indifferent. Nothing has been done to interest him in the business and his work, or to make him feel somehow responsible for both. Generally, only wages, and sometimes fear of dismissal, are his motives for achievement.

The 'Working-Community for the Encouragement of Partnership in Industry', founded by Spindler, defines partnership as follows: 'Business partnership is a system of co-operation resulting from an alliance between management and personnel. Its features are, constant attention to human relations, a mutual sense of responsibility, and the division of profits.' So there are three elements in a partnership:

1. Human unity.
2. Disinterested sense of responsibility.
3. Material interest in profits.

By extensive participation in affairs, the social atmosphere is created in which individuality and humanity can awaken and thrive. Besides participation and collaboration, Spindler wants to bind the workers to the business with material ties, by giving them a share in the capital. Spindler calls these ties, social, spiritual, and material, 'shared-enterprise'.

Spindler's expression 'co-entrepreneur', applied to the workers, means that they are involved in the responsibility for the enterprise, and do not confine their activities to the field of performance, as responsible fellow-workers. Here, Spindler has not taken into account the fact that the entrepreneur's and the workers' obligations lie in two very different directions, and should not be mixed. For we are here dealing with the indispensable balance between the intellectual and technical management, and the practical performance of the workers. This natural division of responsibility is founded on the fact that responsibilities can only be shouldered by specialists in that particular field. The function of the entrepreneur and directors is management and is inextricably bound up with responsibility for capital. The workers' responsibility can never extend as far as this. Like many enlightened entrepreneurs today, Spindler accepts his responsibility for capital in the capacity of a trustee. Not the personal ownership of capital, but the administration of it, is one of the higher responsibilities of the entrepreneur.

It is therefore a social and economic error on Spindler's part, to grant his so-called co-entrepreneurs extensive participation in management, and access to the supply of capital. The shared-enterprise contract lists the cases in which the workers are to advise in decisions. Some of these, such as changes in personnel, and alteration of aims, are already, quite rightly, subject to the workers approval. But investment and borrowing are another matter altogether. The right of workers in a shared-enterprise to interfere in these affairs encroaches on the economic sphere, which is the responsibility of the top management. The workers should only be given the right to be kept *informed* of these matters, so long as the security of their job is not involved. In Spindler's enterprise, he does use information as a general method of arousing the workers' social interest in affairs. This encouragement of interest is very important, as all enlightened entrepreneurs appreciate. But of special interest is the particular form of capital sharing which Spindler has granted his workers, in order to increase materially their extensive rights of responsibility and participation.

As Spindler wishes his enterprise to be known as a 'progress society', the agreement, which is only voluntary, stipulates that the workers shall share not only in the business profits, but also in the assets. A maximum share is 25 per cent. This is effected by a reserve fund being formed from the workers' share. So the workers do not share in the original capital, but hand back part of their share in the profits, to supplement the business capital. This is paid back to the worker when he retires. The capital structure is thus increased, while the actual nucleus of capital, in the form of shares, which really represents the company, remains untouched by the workers.

The sharing of the business capital among the workers has already been customary for a long time in Anglo-Saxon countries. It is usually effected by the abstract method of shares. These do not create social ties, as they appeal solely to the desire for gain. In Spindler's system of a profit reserve fund, there is little appeal to this desire. By this method of building reserve funds, and granting extensive rights of participation in affairs, Spindler is trying to establish a closer unity between the workers and the business as a whole. This raises important questions.

Here, it will pay us to look briefly at America's industrial problems. In America, the Central European social conception of business, with its movement towards the working-community, finds no place. The aims of the American worker are centred on material comfort and inner satisfaction. The need for wider social relationships, which is the deepest need of the East European in particular, but also of the German, and to a lesser extent of the Briton, scarcely appears in the American worker. In the Central European worker, two instincts strive for harmony, material self-interest, and social humanism. He is expected to find some sort of balance between two instincts, and from this to build up an industrial system compatible with human dignity. In America, they have found that human relations help productivity, and therefore profits, and also that these relations cannot be established without giving the workers a share in the profits. However, the American worker is by no means satisfied with mere financial concessions, and Michigan University's Institute for Social Research classifies many kinds of satisfaction which are important to the industrial worker :

1. The satisfaction which the individual gets from a sense of capability.
2. The satisfaction of belonging to an informal group (friends, relations, etc).
3. The satisfaction of being able to identify oneself with a well-known company.
4. The satisfaction of good relations with one's employers.
5. The satisfaction of being able to afford status symbols (cars, fur coats, etc.).

There is also the satisfaction which comes from membership and activity in religious societies, etc.

In this list, the desire for part-ownership in the business is conspicuously lacking. It is evidently not an essential factor. Neither is participation in industrial affairs, at least, not in the German way.

It does exist, however, in the Trade Unions' interference in management, but only in the fields of productivity and wage security, and sometimes in the field of finance. Although the

German Unions aspire to participation in management, there is a basic difference between the German and American forms of participation. Closer examination reveals that while financial interest apparently prevails in the German demands for participation, the real motive is desire for social reform.

From all this, we can conclude that the sharing out of capital is not essential to the development of a feeling of partnership in the workers. Rather is the reverse true, that a sufficiently deep social involvement of the workers in the affairs of the business tends to make them want certain ties of ownership with regard to the means of production. These ties of ownership have nothing to do with Spindler's system or a profit reserve fund. This is only a way of supplementing their wages, and a superficial, purely financial bond between the workers and the business. Spindler himself remarks that 'the frequency and amount of payments have no real influence on the workers' attitude towards the *idea*, that is, the social aim of the partnership. This is an important discovery, because many businesses take great pains to make the idea of partnership popular by frequent distribution of profit shares or premiums. Any good resulting from this is deceptive, as the disadvantages show.'

It is of far greater importance to Spindler's staff, that he has taken the first step towards neutralization of capital. Of course, he has not taken the final step. But, like many other entrepreneurs, he shows a changed attitude to the concept of ownership, by the fact that he looks on himself as a trustee, responsible for his enterprise, its invested capital, and its machinery. A trustee is a legally responsible person, who manages someone else's affairs as though they were his own, in the interests of that person—in Spindler's case, in the interests of all his employees, and of the needs of the economic system. Therefore, Spindler extends his administrative responsibility for his enterprise not only to his relations with his workers, but to the public.

Business management motivated by a disinterested spirit of stewardship, and working in the service of the public, and for the material security of the workers, is the foundation on which partnership and the higher social stages can be built. Its aim is to make the workers recognized as free individuals in business, and to induce them to work as such. But the method of partnership can only partly attain this goal of developing the worker's personality. A partnership like Spindler's certainly creates a social atmosphere, and gives the workers the vital food which enables them to shoulder responsibility—up to a certain point. But this responsibility has to stop short of the entrepreneur's authority, which has, of its own free will, given them this partnership system. In other words, the first move does not come from the workers themselves, and the efforts they do make can therefore only be made within the limits allowed by this system and its head, the entrepreneur. This superior authority of the entrepreneur is expressed in the word *co*-entrepreneur applied to the workers. This means that the entrepreneur has an independent importance, and that the workers only participate. Social equality between the management and workers is thus not yet achieved. This is also shown by the workers' exaggerated claims for responsibility in fields in which they cannot have the necessary knowledge.

So it is not surprising, that Spindler has now concluded that the workers' need for partnership and participation is, at bottom, slight. He writes, 'It is difficult to answer the question, to what degree partnership meets a genuine social need. The idea of partnership can be variously understood. Women usually pay more attention to the short-term material advantages. Men under 30 are also generally more interested in the material side than the social. All partnership businesses agree in reporting that their skilled workers, between 30 and 55, are most actively interested. Among these, those most interested in the social idea consider the material advantages to be incidental, and vice versa. In a personnel, one-third women, two-thirds men, after ten years of the partnership system, 25 per cent are actively interested. The rest are fellow-travellers.'

There will always be fellow-travellers, because a certain proportion of people are always too comfortable to make an effort, or take responsibility. But in Spindler's partnership, the percentage is obviously too great. This is because partnership is a stage below the associative enterprise in social development. Also, wage tensions have not yet been properly eliminated, although the partnership system relaxes them. The wage-earner in a partnership can feel that his own pay is in a way due to the concentrated efforts of all the workers.

In the partnership system, there are still the following shortcomings. Spindler has not yet brought himself to renounce the capital, by objective neutralization. His business has not yet achieved social objectivity. It is still 'his' business, although his attitude of stewardship is a step towards neutralization. Secondly, the partnership system comes to the workers as a gift on the part of the entrepreneur. His first efforts are not met half-way by the workers themselves, although Spindler's ideal tends this way. For he thinks the entrepreneur has a disinterested duty to help the workers who are ready for it to develop complete personalities, to take responsibility, and to look on the business as their concern. By his methods, he can only achieve this to a limited degree, because the basic structure of his business is still capitalistic. But if it *were* achieved, the workers could then begin to feel a sense of socially creative responsibility. But then they would stop trying to become co-entrepreneurs, for management is the sphere of their opposite partner, the entrepreneur. Instead, they would work towards a common responsibility for *performance*. But this is only possible when the essential social ties have been created in a business. For this highest stage of socialization, the system of business-integration paves the way.

Partnership, however, institutes in every case a social inter-dependency between the participants, in their relationship to the business. They encounter one another as equals in the course of business, and this puts a stop to the arbitrary authority of one party over the other. The partners recognize one another's human equality, and have equal rights with regard to each other and to the business. Only in this sense are they partners. Such social conditions of partnership can be seen in the historical idea of democracy. Democracy has brought about political conditions in which downtrodden classes have won equal rights. In industry, such a battle was fought by the Trade Unions. It could win only a theoretical equality, and a comparative participation in affairs. This participation is also an ingredient of wider industrial partnerships, such as today are advocated by the building industry. This is on a higher plane than that of business. Such wider partnerships, it is thought, will change the labour battles into equitable negotiations, by which some mutually satisfactory agreement can be made in regard to wages and working hours. All this, however, produces no partnership in the sense of a human tie to the business and its affairs. But such a partnership is being aimed at in the attempts of enlightened entrepreneurs. A particularly impressive instance of such an attempt is the Spedan Lewis Partnership in England.

THE G. L. REXROTH IRONWORKS

Another partnership business deserves our attention, where the socializing element of co-operation has been outstandingly successful. This is the G. L. Rexroth Ironworks in Lohr, which employs 1,200 workers and clerks. Rexroth has a very clear conception of the deeper factors in labour problems, and of their solution. He says that owing to the dehumanization of industry by mechanization and automation, and the resulting estrangement of the workers from their work, an important part of the workers' individual potentialities remains untapped, and calls forth a deep sense of frustration. 'As the individual is always seeking to become a *whole* personality, and cannot go through the day without secret mental activity, his desires lead a secret life of which he becomes less and less conscious. The part played by antipathy, negativeness, opposition on principle, distrust, is well-known. The working atmosphere, a vacillation between agreement and refusal, is completely unreliable. Uncomprehended, almost incomprehensible involvements and combinations of individual circumstances lie at the bottom of all this.' Business unites people with different destinies. But it also gives the head of the business an opportunity to take upon himself the role of shaping its destiny.

Therefore, Rexroth has for years endeavoured to realize his ideal. He began, as often happens, by improving the wage concept by giving shares in the profits. This was so managed, that the employees, raised to the status of collaborators, *not* co-entrepreneurs, could feel their wages to be fair. But this was still not enough to build a human element in the partnership. So in the course of time, more and more attention was paid to human relations. This was done through the development of social and discussion groups. Besides the board of directors and the industrial committee, a partnership committee and a series of special boards were formed, which are completely free to negotiate all questions of business. 'The function of negotiation,' says Rexroth, 'may be of greater importance to the end goal than to the matter under negotiation.' By this continual endeavour for agreement, con-

F

fidence is created, and business co-operation is made to transcend all personal feelings. Thus, a good atmosphere has been produced. An inquiry into business policies, held in 1961, showed that 75 per cent of the Rexroth employees approved of the Partnership, and 79 per cent acknowledged the fairness of wages, and preferred the business to any other.

It can be said that the partnership concept could be the starting-point for the higher stages of integration and association. For it has succeeded to a great extent in interesting the workers in the enterprise, and creating the necessary elements for a sense of responsibility. Confidence and responsibility are the main ideals of the initiators of this concept.

Our criticism here, as with Spindler, is that this sort of partnership is still too self-sufficient. The Rexroth business has become a great self-supporting community, which sets the whole of the profits to its own account, and shares it all among its members. In the improved wage system, work is paid by a standard wage, and supplemented by bonuses according to the amount of profits. The profits remaining, after payment of wages and salaries, are set aside. These profits consist of the special profits due to extra effort on the part of the workers and management, the special profits due to a boom on the market, and the special profits due to technical progress. I call all these profits free capital formation, and repeat that they should not go directly into the hands of the enterprise and its employees. As long as business relations are based on wage interest, this will be difficult to avoid. On the other hand, it must also be understood that the special profits due to extra efforts at co-operation justify their creators, the workers and management, in claiming a share of them. To what extent such claims are tenable, has already been explained, and will be illustrated in the following examples of associative business.

THE ASSOCIATIVE BUSINESS—INTEGRATION OF SCOTT BADER AND CO.

The social concept of business is characterized in all its stages by the relationship between management and workers, and further by the relationship of both parties to the business. These two relationships, the social-human and the social-technical, take a different form in associative business from what they do in the partnership. The entrepreneur's relationship to the business leads to a special concept of capital ownership, while the workers' relationship to it leads to a higher sense of responsibility. To get a clear picture of such an associative business, let us take a look at an English company.

In England, sixteen years ago, through the initiative of a progressive entrepreneur, a plastics business took on a form of collaboration between management and workers which should be considered as the penultimate step towards a true social order. The Scott Bader company in Wollaston neutralized its capital by transferring it to an independent registered charity organization, the Scott Bader Commonwealth. All profits go to the Commonwealth which is managed by its members. The Commonwealth is open to all employees after two years employment provided they accept certain responsibilities. The Commonwealth disposes of the profits and the additions to capital which these represent. In this Commonwealth, the entrepreneur and the business directors have no more say than the individual worker. It is their common responsibility to decide how the profits shall be divided. So that this can be done in a socially and economically reasonable fashion, the workers have for years been educated on the problems arising in such decisions. Only thus could the members of the Commonwealth bring a heightened sense of responsibility to their decisions on the disposal of capital. Although a bonus is shared among the workers, the feeling has been awoken that it is essential for part of the profits to be used for cultural purposes, and part for charitable work in the locality. Besides this, of course, it is decided how much shall be used for investment. The State levies its portion through taxes.

The Scott Bader Commonwealth is thus naturally subject to certain conditions, which were mutually agreed on and formulated. As security, a council of seven trustees was formed, whose sole concern is to see that the Commonwealth's decisions conform to the spirit and ideal which produced the Commonwealth. There should be such trustees in every business alliance based on co-operation between management and staff, so as to prevent abuses.

We will not say that this sort of communal administration of a business is conclusive in itself, because the question of a correct income structure cannot be solved on this narrow basis. But in such a step as the Scott Bader Company has taken can be seen the promising beginning of a new industrial order at the level of the enterprise. To estimate how such a business system affects the workers, it should be mentioned that recently a committee was formed at Scott Bader's without any instigation from the management. About eight workers got together of their own accord, and held a monthly or fortnightly meeting, for the purpose of making practical decisions on individual technical points brought up by any of the members. According to the minutes of these meetings, it is by a profusion of small measures that the workers take responsibility for production and labour. Such a body can be considered the beginning of a regular works council, set up by the workers' *own initiative*. It has not yet reached the stage of a fully developed production responsible work team, but it is a definite step in that direction. It should be interesting for entrepreneurs, as well as the Trade Unions, to consider this committee carefully.

But it must not be forgotten, that the most important prerequisite for the creation of a committee by the workers' own initiative, is the neutralization of capital ownership and of profits. It would set a most useful example, if the Unions were to include neutral administrative boards in their programme. If these were further developed, they would then form a real foundation for the establishment of a proper wages structure. Fair wages are economic and social sums which can only be fixed by a wider authority than business. There have always been those who have demanded the principle of wage equality. In our times, such a principle can only apply to the *basic* living wage of every citizen. But besides this, it is necessary to grade wages according to the part the individual plays in supporting and developing the community. This would also hold good in the individual working-community, which must develop the awareness that the employee's wages must be graded according to the extent of his responsibilities. The details, then, of the wages system in a business, especially the management's salaries, must be agreed on by all members of the business. Here, an important social problem is touched on, which today lies behind all labour disputes. The competition for increased incomes is due to the repulsive features of the Western system of economy, and reveals this system's essentially anti-social nature in its full blatancy.

If a real working-community is successfully established, the personal salaries of the entrepreneur and directors will not be levelled down. Their special height will be accepted willingly, when the social laws of the income structure are properly understood, and in their practice complete honesty prevails. The entrepreneur's salary is a special case. His equivalent of performance is mainly creative mental effort, and heavy responsibility. These cannot be priced. What the entrepreneur receives as his genuine salary is subject to the same conditions as the salaries of those who are creative in the cultural sphere. His achievements cannot be calculated according to time or quantity. It may seem strange, but in this field there is no other course than for the industrial leaders themselves to decide what they are justified in claiming, fully taking into account the financial state of the business. They can also, on grounds of their *creative* function, claim part of the national capital, the creation of which was originally due to education and culture. The workers must understand this. If they really think, they will then realize that those who bear the final responsibility for the enterprise, on whom its existence depends, and who must also make a special effort to extend the system to industry in general, may also have special financial claims. Apart from this, experience has further shown that when the workers are not involved in rivalry with the entrepreneur, they are not very interested in the size of his salary. This can be seen in the case of civil servants, who do not upset themselves over the ministers' salaries. It is enough if the workers are convinced that the wages structure is fair, and that economic and social factors have been taken into account.

We have three reasons for taking Bader's enterprise as an example of an associative business, albeit an imperfect one. Firstly, the workers themselves have shown initiative, though not at the very beginning, and only to a certain extent. Secondly, the original entrepreneur has renounced his right to private ownership of capital. Thirdly, arrangement has been made for the achievement of a proper wages system and the proper utilization of profits, according to the mutual agreement of all the members of the business. These three factors are inextricably interwoven. Yet even they are not sufficient to produce a perfect working-community, which realizes the principle of association in every detail. To produce this, the entire responsibility for the performance side must be voluntarily shouldered by the workers as a whole. In the perfect business association, nothing more is done directly *for* the workers, but they themselves initiate everything necessary to the business and to their own economic and social needs. The realization of this highest social stage will be impossible, so long as the workers remain passive, and the questions of the private ownership of the capital and a just wages structure remain unsolved. And so long as this is the case, we will continue to hear the aggressive demands of the Trade Unions for an increase of wages, on principle, a share in profits, and participation in all spheres of business. Only an associative form of business can remove their grounds for complaint. Bader's system is still not perfect. It is, of course, hampered by human failings and by the existing laws, which support the mercenary system of commerce.

Another condition for the realization of a working-community is that the workers are able to develop the desire to accept the responsibilities laid on them. They can only do this, if they can feel a real interest in the business, and a real sense of unity with it, arising from the realization that it supports them. To make this possible, all elements of compulsion and autocracy must disappear from the management. Only the moral power of technical responsibility for the whole must remain. The real authority of the entrepreneur is based on this. Bader has done away with the material element of power connected with private ownership of capital, by giving up all personal rights to it. He neutralized it by an institution recognized by law. The Scott Bader Commonwealth is the legal owner of the entire business capital and profits. Socially considered, this foundation is a trust. The individual representatives of this trust are all the employees of the Scott Bader factory who wish to be members. This method of neutralizing capital is practical, though another method might be used. However, the important result of this step was the realization that individual property among the workers is not essential for the development of an associative enterprise. It is generally only a formality, which, especially when it is given as 'shares', contributes only slightly to a firmer unity between the workers and the business, and to the security of their jobs, a security which the entrepreneur enjoys through his possession of capital. This security must be given to the workers by the equalizing of management and workers. The first step towards this is that the entrepreneur gives up his personal rights to capital, as far as material advantages are concerned. His authority in the business management remains undiminished. He must only keep his hands off the material profits. *How* he does this, in other words, how he neutralizes the capital, is not so important.

What is important, is the effect this renunciation of the ownership of capital has on the workers. They no longer need to feel that they are working for the entrepreneur and his private interests. The knowledge that the business does not belong to the entrepreneur or the capitalists opens a gate by which the worker can really enter the business, and if the conditions are right, he can feel the business to be part of his personal life. In a real community, the workers begin to feel so much at one with the business that they become possessive towards it, but do not need to qualify this possession formally. As things are at present with the modern worker, this deeper unity with the business can only be valued by the older workers, as Spindler discovered. The younger ones do not wish to settle down yet. This is due to their growing consciousness of individuality, and its urge for freedom. But the commercial concept of business encourages this restless drifting, as it only understands the hold of payment which a business has over the worker.

ASSOCIATIVE ENTERPRISE AND ASSOCIATIVE ECONOMY

It must be pointed out, that the business association described here is different from the economic associations which the *three-fold* nature of the social system demands for its proper functioning.

In an economic system which has reached the stage of self-government, economic co-operation is achieved by associative alliances between *producers, merchants,* and *consumers.* These associations, involving all fields of industry, serve to further agreement between opposite spheres of interest, but do not possess that high quality of human unity which the associative business aspires to. In the context of the individual firm, of production or commerce, the principle of association has the effect that initiatives for managing and for working, shouldered by two different sorts of people, are taken co-operatively for the highest good of the enterprise. They decide together the various responsibilities of the workers, and the economically and socially correct use of profits, in a manner which is recognized to be fair. This willing co-opera- tion is necessary in business, and natural socially, while the opposi- tion of employer and employee is unnatural, and harmful to industry. Industry, by its very nature, is essentially based on co- operation, in the wider spheres as well as in the individual busi- ness. Associative union between business personnel delves more deeply into the purely human element than is necessary in associa- tions in the wider sphere of economy. The common administra- tion of respective responsibilities, which develops in the associative business, can be considered to be a higher stage of association than the more comprehensive economic associations. The latter extend to *national* co-operation, and are motivated by the same impartial desire for mutual agreement, but the negotiators come and go, while in the individual business, the idea is to develop a common desire for *lasting* unity and co-operation. Both in individual and in national associations, the members encounter one another as individuals in their own right, and try to come to terms for the common good.

THE 'DEMOCRATIC' PRINCIPLE IN INDUSTRY

The head of the Scott Bader factory has founded a special society for the propagation of his social business system. This is the 'Demintry' Society for Democratic Integration in Industry. Integration here means, first, the social alliance between manage- ment and workers, and second, the integrating spirit of compro- mise and co-operation. The application of the political term 'democracy' to such a system is only partly correct.

The Greek word 'kratos' means power, or force. The develop- ment of power is essential to the State. In the struggle for political power, democracy has arisen. Before, political power was in the hands of an authoritarian, often despotic monarchy. The people, the 'demos', overthrew this authoritarian power in the French Revolution, with the intention of establishing the State, in other words, themselves, as supreme authority. Thus it came about that autocracy was supplanted. The people took it into their own hands. Such a rule of the people can take various forms, ranging from a parliament, with so-called constitutional monarchy, to a republic. The republic combines independent rule with representation by the people. Even a republic needs some sort of head. This is answered by a parliament representing the people.

In industry, there was an apparently similar development. Here, power was wielded by an authoritarian, often tyrannical employer. The industrial equivalent of the 'demos', the 'people' is the workers, who are only one section of the People. The workers clamoured for participation in industrial affairs. To get this, they formed Trade Unions, thus establishing an instrument of power. The case would appear to resemble that of the political sphere. But this apparent similarity is due to the fact that the original economic function of the entrepreneur has become associated with a social *power*. This power is exercised not only in the competition for supremacy on the market, but also in the ethical field. This field concerns the recruiting of workers, and the appropriation of profits.

In industry, it is not really a question of power or compulsion, but of collaboration. Therefore, the word 'democratic' does not apply. I prefer the word 'federative'. In industry, the question is one of co-operation and division of responsibility. Final responsibility lies with the entrepreneur. He cannot control by physical power, but by moral power. But political power is arbitrary, and aims at bringing about a certain state of society by compulsion. Another difference is that industrial leaders are not publicly elected, as political leaders are, because the general public have no authority in industry. The workers do not care about choosing their leaders. They only want to put an end to the personal capitalistic power of the entrepreneur, by developing an opposing power, participation in all business affairs. In the commercially run business, such a movement might be called democratic. But in a true social enterprise, such pseudo-democratic activity becomes pointless.

In industry, therefore, political democracy applies only to the commercial business concept, which is based on individual power. It is through sales competition and labour disputes, that power has become a regular feature of industry. The policy of market economy relies on these rivalries, which are a foreign body in the economic system, and injurious to productivity. Businesses are degraded to the state of rival political parties. This unnatural situation can only be overcome by the principle of co-operation.

On whatever lines a business may be run, there is always a

legal side to it. This side does not concern the constitution of power, but the decency of working-conditions. The State supervises society. In business, too, people live together socially, and their relations must be properly organized and controlled. Work itself is governed by the technical laws of production or trade. But this work, which is carried out co-operatively, is bound up with human relations. The social conditions under which it is done include the length of working hours, the time of starting breaks, accommodation, sanitation, safety precautions, first aid, etc. This side of the business is of a legal nature, and calls for proper control, which may involve certain social forms of political democratic methods. This control may be either authoritarian, or federative, that is, with the help of the workers themselves. There are various stages of the latter system. The workers may be consulted, or they may make independent decisions on individual points, e.g. the time to start work. Such details can be settled by the democratic method of a majority vote. This is reasonable, for the human side of labour is a social concern, not an economic one.

In this social field, there may be matters which can be left entirely to the workers' judgment, such as health-insurance, excursions, etc. This federative method of social control must not be confused with the organization of work into spheres of responsibility. These range from the entrepreneur's responsibility for the whole, to the workers' joint or individual responsibility for performance, and to the special communal responsibility of the workers in a working-community. In the case of responsibility, there can be no federative voting, but only delegation by the management and acceptance by the workers.

In political democracy, the people delegate political power and legal administration to their government. But in business, it is the other way round. The administrators, who shoulder the heaviest responsibility, delegate responsibility for performance to the workers, though this responsibility is not comparable with that of government. Responsibility cannot be forced on anyone, for it is a moral power of leadership, and those who accept it must do so willingly. The more a business approaches the final stage of a community, the more the desire of the workers for independent responsibility will make them ready to accept the responsibilities assigned to them by the management. In the network of responsibilities, moral authority is divided on a descending scale. This moral power organizes the physical forces of industry which operate the workers and the machines. Successful co-operation between these moral and physical powers depends on the human solidarity of all members of the business.

Whether, and how far, confidence between workers and management must be ratified by the political method of voting, will then depend on the depth of mutual understanding between the two parties. The acceptance of the entrepreneur by a majority vote is fundamentally out of keeping with the idea of a working-community. This demands unanimity, at least as far as the acceptance or rejection of the man himself is concerned, and not just one aspect of his conduct. Clearly, any criticism of sins or omissions on the part of the entrepreneur calls for a very competent judge.

How this can be managed in practice is shown by the Scott Bader Commonwealth. There, a very interesting rule was laid down, by which the directors of the business are made subject to judgment and control. This control is not exercised by the company, but by the Commonwealth which owns the shares of the company. In the Commonwealth, there is a panel of representatives and a board of trustees. The procedure of judging the conduct of the business management is surrounded by all kinds of safeguards. The twelve representatives are chosen by lot, at the annual meeting, from the members of the Commonwealth. The panel is formed for the purpose of expressing the feeling within the community whether the Board deserves to be given a vote of confidence to continue in office for the ensuing year. If such a vote is withheld then another general meeting is held within three months and a new panel appointed by the same method as before. If confidence is still not accorded, then the trustees are brought in. They examine the grounds for rejection, and submit suggestions for improvement. Among the trustees are people who are not members of the business or the Commonwealth, but are chosen for their special knowledge.

It is one of their functions to clear up the ethical question of whether the directors are to be allowed to continue in their line of policy, or not. The function of the directors is economic, but their position in the enterprise as a whole is a legal one. The Scott Bader Commonwealth is a purely legal institution, not an economic one. Its main duty is therefore the rightful disposal of the profits earned by Scott Bader and Co. Ltd.

This leads to another range of ethical problems which crop up in industry and can be partly solved in the business. In the utilization of business profits, which are gained by a combination of capital, management, and workers, the question of a just distribution of income comes first, and then the question of the proper disposal of the profits left over after the wages are paid. Should they go to investment, education, or the workers? From the entrepreneur's selfish appropriation of the profits has arisen the workers' democratic aggression, since traditional law gives the entrepreneur and capitalists sole right of possession. The Unions' clamour for participation in affairs is also due to the entrepreneur's illogical personal power. This aggression is itself an industrial anomaly, and produces a battle for power, not on economic grounds, but on social ones. The natural thing would be to make objective decision on the disposal of profits, of which every right-thinking person could approve. Such decisions may be made by individuals or committees. The individual entrepreneur could also make right decisions here, but he is not forced to do this. However, in a group composed of entrepreneur, employees and trustees on a basis of equality it is necessary that an agreement is reached regarding the proper allocation of profits. Co-operation of this sort is federative. In certain cases, voting would be necessary, for instance, when it is a question of whether a certain sum set by for culture shall go to education or to the theatre. Here, the federative method is driven to the last resort of voting, because a unanimous decision cannot be reached.

We must therefore distinguish between the unjustifiable *democratic* element in industry and the justifiable *federative* element. History shows that democracy tends towards destructive militancy, while federation aims at creative co-operation. The Trade Unions' demands for participation are mainly democratic. The development of co-operation on the basis of equality between management and workers tends towards federative co-operation. Examples of this are Scott Bader, and others yet to be described.

The word 'federative' is not used politically here, but applies to method. Politically, the term is used for national union between several independent States. However, when it is meant non-politically, it describes a certain method of administration, in any general context, involving mutual agreement. On an equal footing, societies or individuals co-operate, either passively, through a court which they pledge themselves to support, or actively, from their own initiative. The latter is the case when entrepreneur and workers co-operate on an equal footing. The lowest stage of federal co-operation is found in the exchange of ideas, in consultations. In higher stages, it is a question of agreement or mutual decisions. This depends on the subject under discussion. The nearer a business approaches the associative stage, the more agreement there will be between the management and workers on the question of division of responsibility. In federal decisions, voting is possible, but it is out of keeping with the spirit of federation. Unanimity is the ideal of federal co-operation. Voting is therefore a last resort. But in political *democracy*, it plays a large part.

The differences between democracy and federation must be clearly understood, in order to grasp the fact that democracy is not a regular principle in a self-governing industrial system. It is only a transitory phenomenon, that the workers now feel they must interfere in the entrepreneur's responsibilities. They have not yet gained social equality with the entrepreneur. As long as one party has social superiority, no negotiation can bring about the federal administration of industry. Only the democratic principle of participation will prevail, a principle which springs from the underprivileged part of the community. The federal principle demands co-operation, rather than participation. Co-operation is not a question of participation on decisions, but of mutual decisions. However, unlike participation, which interferes in all fields of economy, federative decisions only deal with the *social* questions of business, concerning regulations and the utilization of profits.

Through the institution of a special body to solve the social problems which arise from capital ownership and administration of profits, a great enlightenment comes about in an enterprise. The social side of industry is thereby recognized, and given an organizational expression of its own. But this can only happen within the context of a proper wages structure. This alone makes it possible for federal societies to be organized, like the Bader Commonwealth, which has the legal power to decide how profits shall be divided. If, however, solutions to the questions of capital ownership and a just distribution of income are sought by the method of participation in all spheres of economy, which is the policy of the Unions, then the economic side is being mixed up with the ethical side, with injurious results. It is, however, a reaction against the policy of the commercially run business. There, the ethical questions of profit disposal are determined by private interest, and thus become questions of personal power. It is on these grounds that the democratic desire for a voice in all business affairs is being forcibly put forward. It is injurious to business economy, but it is an expression of the unsolved social question of the ethical division of profits.

For purely economic problems, the business foundations for social administration are not directly responsible, as long as these problems do not concern the workers' welfare, which rarely happens in an associative business. There, economic decisions are the responsibility of the management. In a constitutional monarchy, the king is responsible for a number of decisions. In the same way, the management is responsible for the question of expansion, etc. In this field, the workers are not qualified to judge. Therefore, the federal self-government of a business, extending to social questions, stops short at the most important economic decisions. To leave vital economic problems to federal administration is expecting too much of the workers. This can lead to difficulties which cannot satisfactorily be solved by a majority vote. Where there is a minority which opposes the economic decisions of the management, voting will only make this apparent but not resolve it. The minority will continue to feel dissatisfied, and this is scarcely conducive to a feeling of unity in the factory. The federal principle really only applies to the social-ethical administration of the business. This is not compatible with voting, except on minor points.

Bader has taken the first decisive step towards a business association, in relinquishing his claims to private capital and instituting an acceptable wages system. This ethical basis of production was incorporated in its own right in the Commonwealth institution, thus drawing a clear division between the social side of business and the economic side. The principal social institutions of Bader's enterprise have led to the separation of work from wage interest. Since 1963, no distinction has been made between wages and salaries. Both these payments are entered as wages. In the accounts, their sum figures as a component of the general marginal profits. After deduction of the wages and special expenses, the clear profits are left. This system cannot yet count as a *complete* elimination of 'wage' relations, as such. But the change is so definite, compared with the old method of accounting, that Bader writes, 'It will be a long time before they get used to it'.

Bader places such importance on the independence of the social-federal side of business relations, that he has founded the 'Demintry' Society for the propagation of this idea. It was this that made me go into the relationship of democracy to industry. Considering the differences between democracy and federation, 'Demintry' would more correctly be called a Society for *Associated* Integration in Industry.

THE JOHN LEWIS PARTNERSHIP, LONDON

Of especial interest is the John Lewis Partnership, both for its ideological structure and its social effects. The external structure is very similar to that of the Bader Commonwealth, although Bader's is based on manufacture, while John Spedan Lewis' was founded on trade, a large department store with branches throughout England. Bader's factory employs about 300 workers, Lewis' company today employs more than 16,000. Bader's first step, the neutralization of capital, was in 1948. Spedan Lewis founded his Partnership in 1929, but changed it radically in 1950. Bader revised his Commonwealth in 1963, transferring the entire business capital to the Commonwealth. This was done by Lewis in the beginning, in 1929. But Lewis transferred his capital in the form of a free loan to the Partnership, to be paid back in 30 years, from the surplus profits. After 1950, this capital, now 285 millions pounds, became the *property* of the Partnership.

In both cases, the common factor is that the social movement for neutralization of capital was started by the entrepreneur. Both men showed themselves to be gifted with a high sense of social responsibility. Lewis, at the age of 23, made a discovery about his father's business which shocked his sense of justice. He found out that his father, his brother, and himself together took a profit which exceeded the total earnings of all the workers. That was in 1908. It was 21 years before he could realize his first plans for a partnership, in the face of his father's opposition, and another 21 years before he gave it its final shape. In the accounts of the Partnership, the whole business capital now appeared as the property of the Partnership, in the form of shares.

The Partnership is protected by a trust, the John Lewis Partnership Trust Ltd. It consists of five directors, headed by a chairman. Until his death, this was Lewis himself. This trust controls the administration of the Partnership. With Bader, this control is exercised by the panel of representatives and seven trustees. The Lewis Partnership is managed by twelve directors, the Central Board, which shares authority with the Central Council, chosen from members of the Partnership. The Central Council is not only a working body, but also decides certain questions, which are indicated in the rules. In Bader's Commonwealth, too, there are twelve directors, the Community Council. Lewis' Central Council is the equivalent of Bader's General Meeting of all the workers.

But this structural similarity between Bader's and Lewis' foundations does not mean that their inward nature is the same. There are differences, partly because John Lewis was thoroughly English, while Bader is Swiss, and has brought an element of Central European thought into his system. This will be seen when we compare the social features of both partnerships.

The most interesting thing about the Lewis Partnership is not its technical structure, but its social structure. From the age of 25, Lewis worked continually at the social structure of his Partnership. How he was guided in this by English common-sense is told in his two books, *Partnership for All* and *Fairer Shares*. The latter explains how a social community can be evolved from the natural features of the English character. In human relations, the English demand *fairness*, and in industrial relations, *fair shares*. Lewis divides fair shares into three classes, shared gain, shared knowledge, and shared power.

Shared Gain

Lewis says that it is essential that the worker in a partnership receives earnings that encourage him to do his best for the business. No member, including the management, must have a higher income than is necessary to support him and his family in comfort and decency. But this does not mean that wages must be equal.

Special efforts and great responsibilities must be rewarded accordingly. The maximum wage 'must not be higher than will content the payee, in a world where so many live in poverty'. Next comes the division of profits. Notice that this does not mean *participation* in profits belonging to someone else, but *division* of profits which belong collectively to all members of a partnership.

According to the accounts for 1961/2, Lewis' Partnership gained a clear profit of £2,158,000. After deduction of taxes and payment of other charges, £1,671,000 remained to be divided. Of this, £506,000 went to pension funds, £847,000 as bonuses to the workers. The rest was put into a reserve fund. The bonus was 12 per cent. of the wages, about a month's income. The previous year, it was 14 per cent. Bonuses are paid partly in shares, so that the enterprise can amass investment capital. The rest is paid in cash. The shares are not negotiable. Of the cash, part is used for the common benefit, on sport, culture, and many societies which meet the workers' need for comfort and beauty in their lives. The need for material comfort is deeply rooted in the English, who at one time were responsible for spreading material civilization in the world. If these needs are met, the foundation is laid for the contentment of the English worker. This contentment can be observed by anyone walking round Lewis' stores. The spirit of fairness rules there, and extends to the customers. A typical illustration of this is, that if a customer finds he could have bought an article for less than he paid at Lewis', the difference is refunded at once.

However, Lewis realized that profit sharing alone was not enough to interest the workers in the enterprise itself, or unite them. The two other kinds of sharing aim at doing this.

Shared Knowledge

Here, the purpose is to make everyone personally interested in the business by keeping them informed on all its affairs. Realizing how important it is that every member of the partnership should have a general understanding of the business to which he gives the best part of his life, Lewis tried to develop this understanding in every way. One method is the weekly news-sheet, which not only keeps the workers up-to-date on events, but keeps space for letters, even anonymous ones. This personal contact with every individual in his employ seemed essential to Lewis, since the success of the Partnership to which he had irrevocably made over all his business capital, depended on how happy the members felt in it. Lewis was even of the opinion that it was more important for the social unity of the Partnership that the workers should have a broad understanding of the business, than that they should be given a share of the profits. Free speech, the formation of committees for all possible contingencies, direct contact between management and workers, as many meetings as possible, all this should create understanding and *esprit de corps* among the workers and in their attitude to their work. Such co-operation Lewis calls shared power.

Shared Power

This means the fair and practical division of responsibility in the management of the business, and in administration of the Partnership. Every field of responsibility is a field of moral power. There are fields of varying scope. Individual responsibility or decisions are different from collective responsibility or decisions. Collective decisions can be made either unanimously or by a majority vote.

Lewis seeks to clarify the question of power sharing by the principle of *democracy*. In business, there are responsibilities on various levels. The highest, that of the chairman, is not democratic just because he delegates part of his duties to directors and committees. I have said that the delegation of responsibility to lower levels is not 'democratic'. But the sharing of the highest responsibility among directors on an equal footing could be called 'oligarchic'. However, both terms are far-fetched when applied to industry. Industrial administration does not involve power comparable with that of State government. Also, co-operation between directors on the highest level cannot be compared to the democratic representation of the people in Parliament. On the other hand, this democratic representation of the people does not apply to actual government administration. Here, power ranges downwards. Thus, the highest government authority gains its ends by delegating power to the ministers and other officials beneath it. Only this downward system of delegating political responsibility has its equivalent in business. But neither in politics nor in industry can this system be called democratic. If it were, we would have had industrial democracy ages ago. The exercise of administrative power, in government and in industry, calls for specialized knowledge. Majority decisions are here only possible in matters of detail. Lewis realized this.

Lewis lays great stress on *group* responsibility on the part of the workers, like the production responsible work teams. He thinks such guilds cannot make proper decisions by voting. Unanimity is necessary, and if it cannot be reached, the matter must be decided by a higher authority.

For the private and social contentment of the individual, the proper division of responsibility according to his abilities is without doubt of the utmost importance. However, the business personnel are not only united in the same work, but in the same purpose, that of supporting themselves and one another, by means of the profits. This involves the other side of power sharing. This is the administration of the *Partnership*, and the division of authority in it. In the Partnership, the collective social beliefs of all the partners are the guiding principle, not technical achievement. The Partnership is therefore a legal conception. In Lewis' Partnership, the Central Council, one of the three authorities, is in a sense democratic, since it is elected from the members, as their representative.

The Central Council is endowed with extensive authority. It chooses not only five of the members of the Board of Directors, but three Trustees annually. A sum of 1 per cent of the wages is at the Council's disposal. It is used for settling such social problems as the adjustment of wages to the cost of living, closing-times, family allowances, shortening of working hours, financial help in times of distress, etc. The Council, as representative of the Partnership, also has the right in certain contingencies to submit suggestions to the business management, which is not obliged to accept these, but gives them careful attention. The functions of the Council are delegated among several committees.

All these arrangements, based on Lewis' lifetime of experience, have proved themselves in practice. But it must be remembered that even in the best business systems, there are always a few who are hostile or indifferent, just as the State must always support a certain proportion of delinquents. As entrepreneur, Lewis expected the members of his partnership to serve the enterprise wholeheartedly. In his book *Fairer Shares*, he explains the requirements for membership. 'Anyone who undertakes to devote himself during the day to his work, and in his relations with the enterprise and its members to be at all times sensibly loyal and sincerely amicable, like any partner in an ordinary business.' Without detriment to his high social aspirations, Lewis was very much the business-man, expecting the highest achievements from his staff. Every employee knows that he will lose his job, if he can be replaced by a better worker.

The John Lewis Partnership has now been in existence for more than fifty years. It has survived both wars. Yet the criticism has been made that the whole institution of the Partnership is in the long run based on a spirit of authoritarianism. This is said despite the many rights granted to the members, and the restriction imposed on himself by the entrepreneur, whereby he is subject to the authority of the constitution he himself founded. Yet there *is* an authoritarian element in the Partnership. This is, of course, due to the fact that it was created by the initiative of one man, who had a position of authority in industry. His spirit is still present in the Partnership, as an authoritative power, ruling the whole, and holding it together. His authority was marked by three English characteristics, common sense, fairness, and a practical business sense. Through these traits, Lewis had real power, which has taken the form of a firmly-established system, and which exerts a strong drive over the workers. An entrepreneur can be autocratic in a good sense, as well as in a bad. Lewis indeed showed a thoroughly autocratic nature in his activities. But he used it to establish a social institution, to which he voluntarily sacrificed his business capital.

Purely moral strength always exerts a force of leadership over what it has created. It has authority, but this may be of such a nature that it is willingly obeyed. Lewis, like Bader, aimed at such authority, and achieved it. But let us imagine a partnership or commonwealth system not founded by the initiative of one entrepreneur, but by the workers themselves, who persuade the entrepreneur to neutralize the business profits in a foundation. In this case, the initiative of workers and entrepreneur would have to unite. This alone would produce a perfect social alliance, born of two equal desires. With Lewis and Bader, the workers are placed in the passive role of receivers. They have allowed an ingenious social system to be established among them, and feel cared for by it. It is a convenient, but not infallible solution to the social problems of industry, when the entrepreneur has to create alone what the workers should have joined with him in creating. Bader and Lewis realized that their foundations could not survive, if the workers remained completely *passive* in them, merely enjoying their advantages. Therefore, they have taken the greatest pains to interest the workers *actively*, and to educate them towards an understanding of social self-government, so that from this understanding they may become part of the enterprise. In this field, Bader has made more progress than Lewis.

Bader did not introduce the idea of a Commonwealth until he had educated his workers for ten years. He wanted them gradually to develop understanding and maturity, so that they would want a Commonwealth. Therefore, he also had to make two conditions of membership, the desire to join, and two years' previous service in the company. In Lewis' business, everyone becomes a member of the Partnership from his first day. Thus, he is raised without social or technical preparation to the status of a partner. Yet Lewis gave a great deal of thought to the conditions of membership, considered a trial period, and introduced a scheme whereby a member received higher responsibilities after seven years.

The reason why Bader had better success than Lewis in developing the communal spirit, is not only because of his stricter conditions for membership, but because he has tried to give his Commonwealth a broad ideological basis of human unity. He was inspired in this by the practical Christianity of the Quakers. He even applied Quakerism to production, so that the factory refuses any order connected with war. But this certainly does not mean that Bader only employs Quakers. The Quaker spirit emanates principally from the entrepreneur, and guides the seven trustees, of which he is one. In the Quaker ideology, great importance is placed on acts of brotherly love, which leads to a principle of fellowship in industrial relations. Thus, Bader's social institution has a more deeply spiritual basis than Lewis'. It is more intimate, more directly human. Therefore, Bader's business has also been able to produce associative societies between the management and workers, such as have been described. Bader himself calls his Commonwealth a co-operative society, and contrasts it with Lewis' Partnership, which he calls a constitutional monarchy, which does not really imply denigration, but only a political classification of its social form.

Compared with associative business, partnership is a looser social bond. In it, there is a sort of theoretical equality of all members, which is expressed in certain social rules and institutions. Partnership is a legal relationship between management and workers, placing them theoretically on an equal footing. According to Lewis, this equality involves the division of profits, knowledge, and authority. But *division* of these is not to be taken literally. The proper division of each varies, in practice, according to the respective abilities of the partners. Thus, the equality of the partnership is not invalidated if profits are not divided exactly equally, or the knowledge of some partners is confined to certain fields, or individual authority varies. Only when purely moral or social issues are at stake, are all members equally responsible for decisions, either through representation, like Lewis' Central Council, or *en masse*, like Bader's General Meeting. Such independently constituted bodies of management could at times reasonably resort to the 'democratic' method of voting.

Of a system like the John Lewis Partnership, we ask, 'How is it that it works so well, to the common satisfaction of all?' Lewis writes, 'Partnership is justice. Better still, it is kindness.' Kindness, combined with fairness, two typical English ideals, are the reason why the Lewis Partnership is so successful in England. For kindness and fairness balance that other English characteristic, hard-headedness in business. The three combined produce sharing of profits, knowledge, and responsibility, thus arousing the workers' interest in the technical and social side of the business.

The division of technical and social responsibilities, especially, is regulated in the partnership by the principle of fairness. Recognition of this is without doubt a cause of the good atmosphere at Lewis'. The average German worker, however, having subtler social desires, would not be satisfied in such a partnership as Lewis'. It is more suited to the English type of mentality.

In Germany, the workers' deepest aspirations have been repressed, through the influence of a mentality of three generations who accepted the idea of competition without the idea of fair play. It is, therefore not accidental that Germany developed the concept of Socialism, which had a world-wide influence, but became distorted by wrong methods, such as nationalization of means of production, and compulsory control of labour by the State. The Eastern bloc took these ideas seriously and was able to do so, because it did not have to deal with people conscious of a desire for individual freedom.

But Western workers, German, British, etc., must fulfil their innate, though varying, needs for community and individuality by a truly communal enterprise. Let us take a look at some examples of progressive entrepreneurs in Germany.

VII

Socialization in Germany

THE VOLKSWAGEN FOUNDATION

Let us first take a brief look at the German Volkswagen Foundation, which is contrary to the laws of justice and economy concerning the neutralization of capital. It is an example of what should *not* be done.

The Volkswagen factory, after the Second World War belonged to no one. This situation continued until 1961, when the factory was finally reorganized. Sixty per cent of the shares were made over to people of moderate means, with preference for the Volkswagen employees, and the rest remained in a Foundation which also received the proceeds of the shares bought. For the purchasers, there was the certain prospect of high market profits and dividends. By using the capital in this way, a progressive economic and social step seemed to have been taken. Economically, it meant that the financial value of Volkswagen was once more put into circulation, and received an artificial existence of its own on the stock-exchange, from which the factory itself did not profit. But the social aspect of the business was not affected at all. The commercial principle remained unaltered. In fact, Volkswagen's mercenary features were emphasized by the selling of shares to the staff.

The transformation of the business into a foundation could have been done according to social rules, if Volkswagen itself had carried this through, without effecting thereby a new issue of capital. It could have established the business capital in shares, to be made over to the Foundation. Thus, the profits of the business would have gone to the Foundation. They could then have been used for the common good. The State would have been relieved of responsibilities for which it is not really qualified.

All this shows that neither economic nor social progress is

made by the mere nationalization and neutralization of capital. This is merely the preliminary requirement for social reform in business. Increased satisfaction with wages and gain is still not social reform. If the Foundation can be justified as a solution to an awkward situation, it must be considered as an economic and social blunder. This consists in the fact that it was founded by the State, and that its capital was raised by an artificially created issue of shares, which has doubled the national expenditure on the factory, without public benefit.

There is the danger that the ministers of finance may take possession of the profits, and use them for their budget needs. The principle of the Foundation, that it shall supplement finance, but only to a limited extent, would thus be contravened. Long-term State planning could be fatal to the basic ideals of the Foundation. Nationalization may result in a Foundation forgetting its original aims, and thus becoming corrupt.

THE STAEDTLER FOUNDATION

The Staedtler pencil factory is a limited liability partnership. The two partners personally responsible have each made over their share in the business to a Foundation for the common good. Every future personally liable partner is pledged to do the same. The capital thus made over, however, is lent by the Foundation to the factory, which pays 4 per cent interest. The revenue of the Foundation consists solely of this interest. All business profits exceeding this interest remain in the business, for development, accident insurance, and the welfare of the workers. The Foundation uses its funds solely for the benefit of the Rudolph Steiner Schools, and the Waldorf School.

The Foundation aims at creating a business system described by Rudolf Steiner, who lays down neutralization of capital as the first requirement, though this is not synonymous with neutralization of the means of production. The Staedtler Foundation does not own the means of production, and has no power to dispose of it, though it does own the monetary value of it. Power of disposal lies in the hands of the liable partners, the business management. Neutralization of the right to dispose of the machinery, etc., is not as a rule sensible. In a socialized business, neutralization of ownership should extend only to the right of use. At Staedtler's, this special right of use has not been introduced, since his business has not yet reached the associative stage.

Through transference to the Foundation, the business capital is protected from abuse. Succession to the management in the Staedtler business has nothing to do with family ties, etc. The entrepreneurs choose the person whom they think most capable of carrying on after them. This conforms to the principle of stewardship over capital and means of production. The practice of this principle makes the workers feel they are not working for the entrepreneur's private interests. They are therefore willing for part of the profits to go directly to education and culture.

Every Staedtler employee is told about the spirit which the management would like to see in the business. This is namely a sense of responsibility towards the business and the rest of the staff. The relationship between subordinates and superiors should be one of confidence, mutual respect, and frankness.

In our search for the conditions of a perfect business system, we must ask whether the Staedtler system can lead to the final stage of perfection? The answer is, that in a perfect working-community, there can be neither superiors nor subordinates. These concepts first arose because the workers, coming from the peasantry, were less advanced in a consciousness of individuality than the more sophisticated entrepreneurs, because they were used to being under compulsion to work and obey. But since then, they have advanced in individuality. The truly socialized business system depends on this sense of individuality, for the workers' acceptance of responsibility and co-operation with the management. It would consist of managing partners and performing partners, not superiors and subordinates. To carry out instructions does not mean to be subordinate, when pride in one's work makes one a free agent.

I do not altogether take exception to the expression '*subordinate*'. It is technically applicable to the worker's lower position of authority in the business. It can even have a more factual basis, if it is understood in terms not of power, but of ability. Here, superiority may be mental, but not social. A similar case is the word '*assistant*'. It, too, is applicable in the general situation today. But in a real working-community, there are no assistants. There are people who help the management by their work, but take no intrinsic share in responsibility for the business. In a working-community, there are only fellow-workers. These are all equal members of the community, which they represent jointly. Their individual responsibility for the business, though technically varied, is *socially* equal. However, since the expression *'fellow-workers'* is usually associated only with the *performing* workers, although the entrepreneur is just as much a worker as they are, the word *'colleagues'* would therefore be a better term for *all* members of the working-community, including the entrepreneur.

The perfect community cannot generally be established when an enterprise is just starting up. In practice, a business is usually started by the entrepreneur, who then looks for people to carry out the physical side of production. These people should then unite to take joint responsibility for their work, in the form of a team, on an equal footing with the entrepreneur.

An ideal community cannot be created by the entrepreneur alone. He can only create the conditions which make its rise possible. He must also educate the workers in their responsibilities. Until they respond, a true community is not possible. Instead, we have superiors and subordinates. Bader's Commonwealth is an attempt to inculcate a sense of responsibility in the workers beginning with a corporate participation in the profits. In his factory, voluntary groups have begun to take responsibility. This is the result of many years of education.

The head of the Staedtler enterprise, Dr. Kreutzer, attaches great importance to this education of the workers. He takes pains to develop in them the spirit of the true working-community. This spirit can be evolved only by the awakening of a sense of individuality, which Kreutzer emphasizes.

He says that the living awareness of joint responsibility, and co-operation, not the inanimate machinery, etc., must create the feeling of kinship. This co-operation can only exist through ownership of the means of production being confined to the right of use. Thus, through common participation in spiritual and material elements, the ideal community can be evolved.

In such a community, Kreutzer says:

1. The worker must be recognized as an individual.
2. His responsibilities must correspond to his abilities.
3. Fairness and frankness must form the prevailing atmosphere.
4. Pride in responsibility and initiative must be felt by every worker, for the welfare of all.

Parts 1 and 3 concern the fundamental requirements, humanity, justice, and honesty. Point 2 concerns the general field of labour organization. Point 4 is not just a condition for, but the very essence of, an ideal working-community.

But how to reach this ideal under present conditions? How can the necessary responsibilities be shouldered? A sense of individual responsibility is all very well for the management. It applies to the workers, too, but it is not enough to develop this alone. In the long run, it becomes associated with wage interest, and with compulsion. Kreutzer's ideal of responsibility for the whole can, on the workers' part, only be achieved *jointly*. This is due to the worker's nature, and his need for fellowship.

Kreutzer is fully aware of the problem of dovetailing responsibilities, and suggests councils to decide this. His main point is that 'the ideal business for the twentieth century is consultative, instead of hierarchical or authoritarian'. This is without doubt the best state that can be achieved by the principle of individual responsibility. But it is not the highest stage, in which the individual responsibility of the entrepreneur, and the joint responsibility of teams of workers, must unite. A business formed on these lines can be the ideal of every individual, entrepreneur or worker.

Although Staedtler's has therefore not yet reached the associative stage, this is not the fault of the management alone. The entrepreneur's efforts can only succeed in proportion to the workers' sympathy, maturity, and desire for co-operative responsibility. The Staedtler business has at any rate succeeded in creating a good atmosphere, and giving some workers a desire for personal responsibility. And from this growing sense of *individuality*, the idea of *communal* responsibility for work will eventually be realized. Until this happens, the wage problem cannot be settled either. This is the case as yet with Bader, and still more so with Spindler, Staedtler, and other reformers. The wage situation continues, and greed for gain is the main motive for work. Yet, through the institution of partnerships, and other steps towards the associative stage, combined with a real recognition of the subtle individuality of every worker, wage tensions are gradually being relaxed or even broken, as the exploitation of labour for private gain is gradually being eliminated.

THE CARL ZEISS FOUNDATION

The Zeiss Foundation is world-famous. In 1889, Ernst Abbe decided to put his business capital into a foundation, which he named after his late partner and friend. It included the Zeiss enterprise and the Schott Glassworks, thus becoming responsible for the administration of two companies.

Abbe was a man of exceptional moral and spiritual powers. His Foundation was a reaction against the commercial concept of business, which offended his sense of justice. Like Lewis, Abbe's conscience was troubled by the ever-increasing wealth his business brought him. He became convinced that the company's profits were the result of the combined efforts of all employees, in other words, the result of co-operation.

The outward structure of a business foundation shows nothing of the social ideals which are put into practice in the business. A foundation enterprise can be run on entirely commercial lines, or it can possess elements of partnership, or it can be a proper working-community.

Organization in the Zeiss factory is based on the wages factor. A clause in the statutes runs, 'In the business, the duties of workers towards the Foundation, to the company, and to all superiors only extends to the work agreed on, and the like'. The wage factor is also directly mentioned.

But in the arrangement of the Zeiss wages system, there is in many respects a special generosity. There are not only various compensations granted, in the event of business disturbances, which may be of longer or shorter duration, but there is also a tendency to introduce hiring for a lifetime. As the profits go into the Foundation, the annual income of the management is controlled, so that it may not be more than ten times the annual wage of an average 24 year old worker. And finally the workers receive part of the business profits, as 'deferred payment', as Abbe called it. This has always meant more than a fortnight's wages extra for each worker, and a whole month's is aimed at. For these extra payments, funds are reserved every month, which, however, are set down in the accounts as expenses. In addition, there are generous pensions, regardable as wage supplements.

Abbe laid down two rules for the Foundation's disposal of the business profits. Firstly, part should go to the workers, as described. Secondly, the profits should help schools, research, and the University of Jena, where Abbe received the education which later helped him to make his great discoveries in the field of optics.

In 1955, the two firms moved to Heidenheim and Oberkochen, and the Foundation could no longer make these donations to culture, since all profits had to clear the debts incurred by rebuilding, etc. Only since 1962 has money been spent once more on scientific research.

THE ROBERT BOSCH TRUST

In 1964, the will of the founder of Robert Bosch Ltd. came into effect. In an enterprise which employs 75,000 people, the capital was put into an existing Trust, which already possessed 2 million pounds. It now received a further 9 million. Since then, the Trust now administers 12 million pounds of the entire capital shares of the firm, which amount to 15 million. The Trust has the right to buy the remaining 3 million from the other shareholders at the current market value. It must pay for these out of the dividends it gets from the shares it holds. Recently, the business has paid 6 per cent dividends, so that the Trust now receives about £750,000 a year. The dividends, apart from the payments for the remaining 3 million shares, are spent entirely on public welfare, as in a foundation. The things Bosch wished to see cared for include medicine, especially homeopathy, education, social services, international understanding and the arts and sciences. His disinterested social nature can be clearly seen in the fact that he put the war profits of the business into various foundations, since he loathed the idea of profiting from war.

Although the assets of the business lie in the Trust, the latter has no administrative power over the business, as it does not possess any voting rights. For the administration of the business a special organization has been created, i.e. the Robert Bosch Industrial Participation Society. Although only possessing a few shares they exercise the power of 60 votes out of a total of 70 votes. The seven members of the Society are prominent people, two directors of the company, and five heads of industry who used to belong to the board of directors. Thus, management of production is kept quite separate from the Trust.

Therefore the whole capital of the firm has been neutralized and is administered by an Independent Trust. This foundation, such a great support to culture, has no direct relation to the business itself, in which 75,000 people are employed.

Like Abbe, Robert Bosch was an entrepreneur who created a world enterprise from a little factory. In his attitude to his workpeople, his main concern was achievement. On the other hand, he felt a great responsibility for the workers' enjoyment of every kind of material security and provision in life. As far as their material desires are concerned, his workers can feel satisfied. Bosch achieved objectively and impersonally what might otherwise be possible by the practice known as paternalism. He thought it very important that he should not be looked on as a benefactor. He did not wish to dominate or patronize his workpeople. He realized that they were free, independent individuals, and should be treated as such. In his opinion, they would not do exceptional work unless he offered them something exceptional in return. He once said, 'I don't pay good wages because I have a lot of money. I have a lot of money because I pay good wages.' Like Lewis, Bosch recognized that everything depended on uniting the workers with one another, with the management, with their work, and with the enterprise. They both realized that good relations and a good atmosphere could not be established without the workers' help. This was to be obtained by freeing the workers from insecurity, and familiarizing them with the business by continual information, such as is given in the Bosch newssheet.

However, Bosch's neutralization of capital does not really lead to social reform of the enterprise. The wage concept continues, although it is modified by many refinements, such as steady employment, continued payment in bad times, generous pensions, care of the bereaved, etc. But all this financial provision does not cover the deeper social needs of the German worker. Bosch wanted to create a working-community. But his methods were inadequate, and he was hindered by a serious obstacle, the fact that German workers are socially uprooted, and have become an isolated class.

SUMMARY OF METHODS OF NEUTRALIZING CAPITAL
AND ADMINISTERING PROFITS

We have discussed so many ways of handling capital, that a systematic summary of concepts of ownership may be helpful.

1. The commercial concept of *capitalism* is based on the entrepreneur's or owner's almost unlimited power over capital and profits. In protest, Socialism would deprive private owners of their capital, and make it a common possession, which is *nationalisation*. This may be considered as neutralization of capital, in so far as the capital is thus removed from the power of the individual. But it is surrendered to a still greater power, the State, for better or for worse.

2. In true neutralization, the use of capital is not determined by the individual, or by the State, but by industrial and social needs, and a corresponding law which protects the capital from any self-interested administration and organizes its practical and fair disposal. Such neutralization makes the entrepreneur's function an unselfish one, and opens the way for ethics in industry. Ownership of capital becomes *trusteeship*. This can be done without legally binding renunciation of capital, if it comes from the entrepreneur's own initiative. Here, neutralization is not bound by legal contract. This is the case with Spindler and Rexroth. They administer their capital as a voluntary trust.

3. The legally binding neutralization of capital is a *Foundation*. The foundation is formally binding, and arranges matters to exclude any struggle for personal gain or industrial power. Its aims always include support of charities, and cultural institutions. Such a foundation may have various forms. For instance, capital and assets may be transferred to it. Besides *Capital or Assets Foundations*, there are Institutional Foundations, where the foundation is responsible for the administration of a school, etc. The school builds funds for the foundation.

The type of foundation mainly concerning us here is the *Management Foundation*. This is solely responsible for the administration of one or more businesses. The authorities may either be themselves members of the business management, or otherwise qualified persons. Complex Foundations arise, when several of these different types of function are contained in one foundation.

The foundation-enterprises we have examined are based on various types of neutralization :

(a) The *partial neutralization of capital* by a *Capital Foundation*, like the Staedtler Foundation. The means of production in the Staedtler factory were not put directly into the Foundation, but part of their value, that is, the invested capital. Donations to the Foundation come from the responsible partners of the company from investment by shareholders and other third parties. The capital thus accumulating in the Foundation is lent to the company for 4 per cent interest. Thus, the *whole* value of the means of production is not in the hands of the foundation, and therefore neither is the whole enterprise. The Foundation, as partial owner of the Staedtler capital, really disposes only of the capital of the personally liable partners. This, together with the enterprise, is thus protected from arguments over succession and inheritance. The cultural concerns of the Foundation have been described.

(b) The Bosch Capital Administration Trust is of the nature of a Financial Foundation. Part of the entrepreneur's resources were handed over to the Trust but not the factories nor the capital equivalent of the whole enterprise. Here, part of the entrepreneurs' resources were put into the Trust, and also the capital value of the enterprise. But the business itself is not administered by it. The Trust thus became the former owner of the enterprise, but only in a narrow sense. The transfer of financial ownership withholds from the Trust important rights of administration. It does not possess the right of disposal, and therefore sale, of the business and title of ownership. Surrender of the right to a voice in the business further deprives the Trust of the right to influence utilization of the means of production. This right, which is part of the right of ownership, has been surrendered to the Bosch Society for Industrial Participation. The Trust retains only the right to the profits from the shares. These go to cultural and social work.

H

The Bosch Trust shows that the charitable and social ends served by the foundation can also be served by a limited company trust. The difference is that the trust must pay a property tax for the assets put into it, while a foundation is immune from this. On the other hand, a foundation is subject to government supervision, from which the limited company is free.

(c) An outstanding example of *complete neutralization of the business and its profits*, through an institution, is the Zeiss Foundation. Such an institution largely depends on its administrator, and the extent of its influence over the business itself. The Zeiss Foundation administers both the industrial and the non-industrial assets. The first are administered by the business management, which is chosen by the Foundation, while the second are administered directly by the Foundation itself. The highest authority responsible for the Foundation's administration is the Minister of Education and Culture. Although the Foundation is under government supervision, it is not subject to political interests, but only to the interests of the enterprise, as agreed on. It appoints the members of the business management, and also a Foundation delegate, usually a prominent figure in industry. He has to see that the statutes are upheld, and to negotiate between the business management and the Foundation authorities. The main features of the Zeiss Works consist of the complete neutralization of both the Zeiss and Schott Companies under one single foundation.

On the subject of 'free' capital formation a final point should be made regarding the proper neutralization of profits. In these the portion which constitutes 'free' capital is lumped together with the amounts needed for ploughback (re-investment), staff bonus and possible dividends to shareholders. In this way it is usually overlooked that neutralization of the profits is carried out indiscriminately. 'Free' capital should be allocated above all for the support of culture, to the influence of which in fairness part of the profits in industry can be traced. If this is not recognized, profits, even in the case of a Trust, may be allocated solely for the benefit of all those working in an enterprise. In such cases neutralization would be prevented through egotism on the part of management and employees. The consequences of such methods of profit and capital distribution would inevitably lead to anti-social isolation and self-sufficiency.

Enterprises where the management, and perhaps the workers, are aware of their duty towards the public, especially culture, make it their business to deduct a portion of the neutralized profits, to be spent on education, research, social welfare, etc. This is the case with Zeiss, Bosch, Bader, and Kreutzer.

The idea of supporting culture directly through industry, without intervention of the State, exists in American industry. It is done through extensive foundations, which even help to support culture in other countries. Such ideas are inspired by the spirit of the times, which would make the creative function independent of the State, so that it might be free to develop. It is essential that industrial workers and leaders get rid of their mercenary attitude, and grow to realize that the needs of culture should be met voluntarily by industry itself. This can only happen when free capital is clearly differentiated from the business profits, separately recorded, and finally neutralized.

Conclusion

Our explorations were meant to make a contribution to the realization that economic life can only take its true form in a new social order. By emphasizing the social-co-operative aspects of the new order we indicate at the same time the precondition for its greatest productivity. We have shown this with reference to the enterprise, the cell of the economy. In the enterprise, in which the closest human co-operation takes place, the social problems of the economic order manifest themselves most immediately. Here the question arises how the work of human beings ought to be integrated into the economic process and how the economically necessary work can be done within humanely true forms of co-operation. This co-operation poses the problem of the human relationships between the two opposites in the organization of the enterprise, the managers and those who execute the work. Both of these must take the initiative for social change if the enterprise is to find its true form. In this book we have explored initiatives which might be taken and their potentialities in the present industrial situation. We have found that the entrepreneurs who wanted to be active in this direction have accomplished much, but they cannot achieve a new order on their own if the workers remain passive. The latter really should take the initiative to satisfy their deeper human needs.

The main obstacle on both sides is a narrow, self-centred attitude. For the entrepreneurs this attitude, combined with their right to ownership of the means of production, leads to personal appropriation of the earnings due to increased productivity resulting from a common effort. This drives most of the workers into an attitude of opposition and accounts for the lack of personal interest in their work and in the economy as a whole. They withdraw into their private lives and live for the enhancement of their standard of living, striving with all their energy for material possessions. This gives them a sense of security through which they attempt to maintain a sense of integrity and meaning. But possessions as such cannot give a true sense of meaning. The workers are therefore called to act creatively in the direction indicated in this book. The real need is for the workers to take responsibility rather than have everyone else—the enterprise, the State, the trade-unions—do everything for them. The latter should do all they possibly can for the workers, but not in a way which strengthens their narrow, self-centred attitudes in such a way as to inhibit their higher aspirations and make them satisfied with a purely biological existence.

These final comments are subject to the qualifications indicated in the text. Their purpose is to strengthen the will, to put into practice our knowledge of the significance of the social aspects of work on the part of management and the workers.

Nothing is so urgently needed in our age as the realization of new social relationships in the economy. Most of the decisions and actions now taken in the economic sphere of life are not imbued by social considerations and have, therefore, ultimately a socially destructive effect.

References

BLUM, FRED H., *Work and Community*, The Scott Bader Commonwealth and the Quest for a New Social Order, London 1968.

FLANDERS, ALLEN, RUTH POMERANZ and JOAN WOODWARD, *Experiment in Industrial Democracy*, A Study of the John Lewis Partnership, London 1968.

GOYDER, GEORGE, *The Future of Private Enterprise*, Oxford 1951

GOYDER, GEORGE, *The Responsible Company*, Oxford 1951.

JAQUES, ELLIOTT, *The Changing Culture of a Factory*, London 1952.

LEWIS, JOHN SPEDAN, *Partnership for All*, Kerr-Gross Publishing, 1948.

LEWIS, JOHN SPEDAN, *Fairer Shares*, Staples Press, 1954.

DE MAN, HENDRIK, *Joy in Work*, London 1929.

ROWNTREE, B. S., *The Human Factor in Business*, London 1938.

SAWTELL, ROGER, *Sharing our Industrial Future?* London 1969.

WEBER, MAX, *The Protestant Ethic and the Spirit of Capitalism*, London 1948.

WILKEN, FOLKERT, *New Forms of Ownership in Industry* with an Introduction by Jayprakash Narayan, Rajghat, 1962.

A list of German books mentioned in or relevant to *The Liberation of Work* may be found in the original German edition entitled *Die Befreiung der Arbeit*, Verlag Die Kommenden, Freiburg. i. Br., 1965.

Note on the author

Professor of Economics (economic theory, industrial relations, social economics, statistics, monetary theory, history of social thought). Born 1890. Ph.D. in political economy, University of Munich 1922. Since 1925 taught at the Universities of Detmold, Dresden and Freiburg. In 1937 declared by the Nazis to be politically not reliable and demoted in academic rank. In 1952 restituted and given a chair as Professor of Economics at the University of Freiburg.

Publications (all in German): *Human Principles of Theory of Value*, Jena 1924; *Theory of Agricultural Prices in Germany 1895-1913*, Berlin 1925; *Health and Illness in Relation to the Cultural Crisis of our Time*, Munich 1925; *The Balance of Economic Life*, Jena 1926; *Principles of an Organic Economy*, Zurich 1934; *History of Ideals with Reference to the German Situation*, Stuttgart 1948; *Autonomous Development of the Economy*, Freiburg 1950.

Index

Abbe, Ernst 95
Action research viii
Advertising 28
American 63, 101
    Entrepreneur 89
    Influence 36
Apathy 3
Armament 27
Awareness 45

Bader, Ernest 68-72, 74, 80, 82, 86, 87, 88, 93
Bingo 2
Bonus 16, 25
Bosch, Robert 96-97
    Trust 99-101
Brentano, Lujo 46

Capital 15-31, 51
    Formation 68
    Neutralization 84-91, 97, 98-101
Character and Work 4
Community 34
    Working 9-10, 21, 33-38, 41, 44
Competition xi, xii
Communism 50
Co-entrepreneur 61, 65
Co-operation 14, 36, 40, 52
Culture 18, 26, 27, 45, 56, 78, 100-101.

Darwin 24
'Demintry' 74, 81
Democracy
    Economic 74-76
    Industrial 46-51, 84-85, 88
    Federative 78, 79
    and Partnership 66, 80
    Political 74-76

Education 29, 45, 56, 78
Employment
    Full 5-7
    Steady 95, 97

Germany
    Social change 90-101
Goethe, Wolfgang 52

Human values 1, 2, 35, 52

Income 12, 15, 16, 29, 21-29
Investment 16, 19, 22-23

Kreutzer, Dr. 93, 94, 101

Law 3-4
Labour-market 1-20, 58
Lewis, John Spedan 81-89
Lewis Partnership 81-89

Market 1, 2
Marx, Karl 2, 5, 11, 33
Marxism 19
Means of production 8-12, 35

Nationalization of industry 46-51, 56, 89, 90-91, 98
Needs 13-14

Organic 9, 10
Ownership 21-29
    of capital 51-52
    Concept of 98-101
    and new social order 55-57
    Part ownership 63-67
    and profits 24
    Utilization 33, 40
    and work community 33

107

Participation 46
   In associative business 73-81
   and democracy 47
   and partnership 60-67
Partnership 60-68
Piece-work 8
Pools 2
Premium Bonds 2
Private enterprise 58-97
Productivity 16-17
   and division of profits 31
   and ownership 33
Profit
   and means of production 19
   Neutralization of 100-101
   and shared enterprise 61, 83
   and sharing 25, 42, 64
   and unearned income 16
   and workers 15

Quakerism 87

Responsibility
   and associative business 69, 76,
      84, 93-94
   Fear of 32
   and human dignity 52
   Sense of 31, 92
   Responsible task force 36
   and shared enterprise 61
   and workers 37-43
Rexroth, G.L. 67-68, 99

Scott Bader Commonwealth 68-73,
   77-82, 85, 88, 93, 101
Security
   and responsibility 33, 41, 102
Seniority 41
Shared enterprise 60-66
Society 42
   Fundamental law 3-4
Solidarity 7
   Functional and social 10
   of workers and management 11,
      30, 46
Spindler, Gert 60-67, 73, 98
Staedtler 91-94, 99

State
   and capitalism 50
   and control of capital 28
   and culture 18
   and distribution of income 14
   and new social order 47-51
   and ownership of capital 22
   and social problems 37
   and social system xiii
Steiner, Rudolf 3, 15, 38, 58, 91
Steiner schools 91
Stockholders 11

Teams responsible for production
   36, 44, 45, 53, 55
Trade Unions xii, 2, 44-57.
   and achievement in work 5
   American 7, 63
   and democracy 66
   and labour force 36
   and power 75, 78
   and profits 23, 37
   and reorganization of industry
      48, 102-103
   and social consciousness 34
   and social reform 44-57, 70, 72
   and wages 15, 39
Trust 98, 100
Trustee 21
   and enterprise 25, 62, 64, 69,
      77-78, 82, 85

United States 53

Volkswagen Foundation 90-91

Wages
   and capital 24-29
   As category of income 41
   and fixed working hours 40
   Investment wages 16
   and labour market 1-20
   and payment for achievement
      41-43
   Structure 54, 71, 79-80
   and work 39, 43

War 96
Work
  meaning of v, 3, 6-7, 67
  motive to 30
  and new social order 46-51
  and satisfaction 63
  and self expression 4
  and wages 39-43
Working community 39-46

Zeiss Foundation 19, 95-96, 100, 101